MW00379987

Introduction

*So teach us to number our days, that we may apply our hearts unto wisdom.—*Psalm 90:12

God designed the Christian life to be a life that reflects His glory, majesty, and wonder. While He didn't promise us that we would never encounter pain or suffering, He did promise that we could experience "fullness of joy" in His presence—we can have a full life!

*Thou wilt shew me the path of life: in thy presence is **fulness of joy; at thy right hand there are pleasures for evermore**.*
—Psalm 16:11

The reality is that we cannot create a wonderful life in our own efforts. The key to having a wonderful life is to fill it with wonderful *days;* and the only way to have wonderful days is to get into the routine of regular fellowship with our Creator through prayer and Bible study.

When we spend time with the Lord, our self-centered concerns are refocused onto the needs of others, our sinful habits are dispersed, our tired souls are renewed, and we begin to reflect and radiate Jesus Christ.

This journal is designed to draw you closer to Christ as you grow spiritually so that you can experience a truly wonderful Christian life.

How to use this journal:

Part One: It's a Wonderful Life—This first section is meant to give biblical instruction that will encourage you to live the life that God intends for you to live as a Christian woman. It begins by addressing the importance of God's Word as spiritual food; which will aide in establishing a time, place, and focus when spending time in the Scriptures. It also covers principles and verses from the Bible that will help deepen your prayer life, enrich relationships, and make memories. I encourage you to spend some time reading this first section to help make the most of your journaling. At the end of this section, you will find Bible reading schedules, a place to write out your prayer list and record God's answers, as well as a section for notes—perhaps for a particular Bible study you may do throughout the year, an outline from a devotional or sermon you found helpful, or personal lists you'd like to keep handy.

Part Two: Giving Your Day a Wonderful Start—The second section is your daily journal as you record what God is teaching you through His Word. Each day, as you spend time with the Lord in the pages of His Word, you'll be prompted to record what God is doing in your life in specific categories.

This journal will be a capsule of the growth God brings in your life over a process of many days. It is our prayer that you would open these pages, fill them with glorious truths that you learn from God's Word, record in them God's goodness and answers to your prayers, and that you would ultimately live an abundant and wonderful life to the glory of Christ.

It's a Wonderful Life Journal

TERRIE CHAPPELL

Copyright © 2016 by Striving Together Publications. All Scripture quotations are taken from the King James Version.

First published in 2016 by Striving Together Publications, a ministry of Lancaster Baptist Church, Lancaster, CA 93535. Striving Together Publications is committed to providing tried, trusted, and proven books that will further equip local churches to carry out the Great Commission. Your comments and suggestions are valued.

All rights reserved. No part of this book may be reproduced, stored in a retrieval system, or transmitted in any form or by any means—electronic, mechanical, photocopy, recording, or otherwise—without written permission of the publisher, except for brief quotations in printed reviews.

Striving Together Publications
4020 E. Lancaster Blvd.
Lancaster, CA 93535
800.201.7748

Cover design by Andrew Jones
Layout by Craig Parker and Jocelyn Allen
Edited by RaKia Harris

The author and publication team have put forth every effort to give proper credit to quotes and thoughts that are not original with the author. It is not our intent to claim originality with any quote or thought that could not readily be tied to an original source.

ISBN 978-1-59894-337-5
Printed in the United States of America

Contents

PART ONE

It's a Wonderful Life

ONE

Nurture Your Soul

Wherefore do ye spend money for that which is not bread? and your labour for that which satisfieth not? hearken diligently unto me, and eat ye that which is good, and let your soul delight itself in fatness. Incline your ear, and come unto me: hear, and your soul shall live; and I will make an everlasting covenant with you, even the sure mercies of David.—ISAIAH 55:2–3

One of the things we must do to stay alive is eat! Along with air, water, and sleep, our bodies need food. The nutrients contained in the food we eat keep us healthy and strong. If we neglect to nourish our physical bodies, our health will inevitably decline. The human soul works the same way. We must regularly feed on God's Word to stay alive and spiritually healthy. We must continually and purposefully nurture our souls with the Word of God. First Peter 2:2 says, *"As newborn babes, desire the sincere milk of the word, that ye may grow thereby."* And Job 23:12 says, *"Neither have I gone back from the commandment of his lips; I have esteemed the words of his mouth more than my necessary food."*

Spending time in Bible reading and prayer are to our spiritual lives what eating and resting are to our physical lives. Obviously, the less we eat and rest, the weaker we become. Even so, the less time we spend with the Lord, the weaker we will become against the attacks of Satan. When we deprive ourselves of the nutrition found in the Bible, the "junk food" of this world becomes dangerously sweet to our spiritual senses. Proverbs 27:7 says, *"The full soul loatheth an honeycomb; but to the hungry soul every bitter thing is sweet."*

Could I ask you, then, how is your spiritual appetite right now? Are you strong in the Lord? Are you hungry for quality time with God? Or, have you been binging on the junk food of this world? Perhaps you are weak, in need of a structured diet to restore your spiritual health. In the following pages, I'd like to share some helps that will increase your spiritual appetite. I invite you to begin (or to continue) the satisfying process of nurturing your soul in the Word of God.

The Right Appetite

Many of us are starving spiritually and we don't even realize it. God designed the human body to trigger a physical desire to eat several times a day and the same is true for our spiritual lives.

An appetite can come naturally or it can be acquired over time. When you became a Christian, the Holy Spirit took up residence in your life and gave birth to new appetites. So, if you don't have a spiritual hunger for the Bible, then one of two things may be wrong.

First, you may be spoiling your appetite. It could be that your spiritual stomach is filled with other things. Many times children, as well as adults, come to a dinner table without an appetite because they've been snacking on junk food. Being full of chips and candy will eliminate any desire for a nutritious meal. As Christians, if we don't have a hunger for Scripture, we too should investigate to see if we have unconfessed sin in our lives or if we are filling our lives with other "foods" that take away our desire for God's Word.

Second, you may not have acquired a taste for the Scriptures. Perhaps your appetite for God's Word is something that needs to be developed. I encourage you to spend time in the Word of God, even if initially you don't feel an overwhelming desire for it. You will find your hunger for it growing as you discover how it satisfies your soul's deepest needs.

Sometimes Christian women think that the Bible knowledge they gain from regular church attendance is enough to fill their appetites. Spending time in God's Word only at church would be like eating only a few pre-prepared meals a week. A spiritual diet consisting solely of what others have prepared for you is like exclusively eating canned food and Lunchables. God wants us to have a home cooked meal, with balanced courses so rich and flavorful that we are left satisfied and eagerly awaiting the next bite. He wants you to spend time personally preparing, tasting, and savoring His Word. When you discover how truly good Bible study "tastes," you will find yourself going back for more.

> *The longer you read the Bible, the more you will like it; it will grow sweeter and sweeter; and the more you get into the spirit of it, the more you will get into the spirit of Christ.*—ROMAINE

Jeremiah 15:16 says, *"Thy words were found, and I did eat them; and thy word was unto me the joy and rejoicing of mine heart: for I am called by thy name, O LORD God of hosts."*

And in Psalm 119:103 we are reminded, *"How sweet are thy words unto my taste! yea, sweeter than honey to my mouth!"*

I challenge you to prove Psalm 34:8, *"O taste and see that the LORD is good: blessed is the man that trusteth in him."*

The Advantages

Here is just a short list of advantages to reading the Word of God:

- It is the way to grow spiritually—1 Peter 2:2; Matthew 4:4
- It is the way to grow in faith—Romans 10:17–18
- It is the way to have victory over sin—Psalm 119:9–12
- It is the "seed" for our witnessing—Luke 8:11; 1 Peter 1:23; Psalm 126:5–6
- It is how our hearts stay tender—Jeremiah 23:29
- It is where we obtain God's wisdom—Psalm 19:7
- It is how the Lord guides us—Psalm 119:105
- It gives instruction in doctrine—2 Timothy 3:16
- It is the way to have great peace—Psalm 119:165
- It is our strength—Psalm 119:28
- It is our assurance of salvation—1 John 5:13
- It is the way to know God's will—Psalm 119:104–105
- It gives us spiritual discernment—Psalm 119:130
- It is the way to be comforted—Psalm 119:52
- It is the way to experience answers to prayer—John 15:7
- It is our hope—Psalm 119:81
- It is the way to find joy—Psalm 119:11
- It leads to true success—Joshua 1:8
- It is the way to know God more intimately—John 1:1

What an encouraging list! There are so many blessings to claim as a result of consistent, meaningful time in God's Word. Don't settle for anything less!

The Appointment

Nurturing your soul is not something that will happen by chance—it must be deliberate. Right now, take a moment to commit to the Lord that you will spend time with Him every day. Set an appointment with God just as you would a doctor's appointment or another appointment on your daily agenda. Establish a time and a place, and determine not to cancel it.

If it is at all feasible, make this appointment the first one of your day. Most health experts agree on one thing—always eat breakfast! We need our spiritual breakfast! If mornings truly aren't the best time for you, then schedule your appointment for later in the day when you feel you can be most attentive. But, as you strive to nurture your soul, it's so helpful to meditate on at least one verse or passage of Scripture before entering into the busyness of your day. It will provide the needed strength and encouragement to get you through your daily schedule. Just as a runner would stretch to prepare his muscles for the endurance of the race, so we must "warm-up" our spiritual muscle, the heart, to prepare for our daily marathon.

After you have assigned a time, establish a place where you can be alone with God. Jesus had a set place to where He resorted when He was on this earth. When Judas betrayed Jesus, he knew exactly where He would be. John 18:2 says, *"And Judas also, which betrayed him, knew the place: for Jesus ofttimes resorted thither with his disciples."* We learn from Daniel's life that he was consistent in praying in his chamber three times a day. Notice the phrase "as he did aforetime" in Daniel 6:10: *"Now when Daniel knew that the writing was signed, he went into his house; and his windows being open in his chamber toward Jerusalem, he kneeled upon his knees three times a day, and prayed, and gave thanks before his God, as he did aforetime."*

In a similar way, when we draw aside to a quiet place to pray, we must block out our busy world and open our hearts to the Father, then our darkened world of disappointments and trials will be illuminated. We will enter into communion with God; we will sense His presence, and we will be assured of His provision for us.

The Approach

It is imperative to our spiritual survival that we are daily in the Word of God. Spurgeon said, "We quickly lose the nourishment and strength of yesterday's bread. We must feed our souls daily upon the manna God has given us." First Timothy 4:13 says, *"Till I come, give attendance to reading...."* Because reading God's Word is a command, we must consistently stick to a plan. While there are some that are best at following a set routine, there are others whose mantra is: "variety is the spice of life." Whatever you prefer, your approach cannot be hit or miss. There are different ways to read God's Word, and you may want to change things up from time to time to keep your devotions fresh and vibrant. Here are a few methods to consider incorporating into your devotional life:

Read God's Word

Vary your approach to reading God's Word. You may want to read the books of the Bible in chronological order or pick a particular book of the Bible to read through several times. There are many different Bible-reading schedules you can follow. (You will find a plan to read the Bible through in a year on pages 49–52 of this journal.)

Study

Determine to intentionally read God's Word to understand the truths inside. There are many ways to study the Bible. Consider doing a word or topical study—defining, memorizing, and applying a particular word or phrase. You may want to focus on different Bible characters or spend time exploring the attributes of God. Decide on a topic for study, and journal what God teaches you. (There is a section of blank notes on pages 75–83 which you could use for such studies.)

Meditate

Meditate means "to ponder or to reflect." God commands us in Joshua 1:8 to meditate on His Word continually. *"This book of the law shall not depart out of thy mouth; but thou shalt meditate therein day and night, that thou mayest observe to do according to all that is written therein: for then thou shalt make thy way prosperous, and then thou shalt have good success."* It's easy to justify our lack of meditation by pointing out our long "to do" list and lack of time. But we all seem to find time to mull over problems and personal situations with which we are dealing. It should be much easier, and is definitely more spiritually building, to mull over the promises of God. We need to absorb what we are learning from God.

George Mueller's testimony gives a wonderful challenge on the meditation of Scripture: "The first evening that I shut myself into my room, to give myself to prayer and meditation over the Scriptures, I learned more in a few hours than I had done during a period of several months previously." When was the last time you "shut yourself into a room" for the sole purpose of meditating on the words and promises of God to you?

There are three key words that can help you in the process of meditating on God's Word:

Visualize—Put yourself in the situation of the story which you are reading. When did this take place? How would I have felt? What circumstances led to this point?

Emphasize—Read the verse, emphasizing each word or phrase.

Memorize—We memorize our phone numbers, social security numbers, bank account numbers, our driver's license numbers, numerous passwords and pin numbers; but how many Bible verses have we committed to memory? Bible memory is a discipline, and unfortunately, it is not practiced enough among Christians. Bible memory allows us to take God's Word with us wherever we go. You may be surprised when verses that have been committed to memory will come to your mind to keep you from sin or to give wisdom for the moment. Psalm 119:11 says, *"Thy word have I hid in mine heart, that I might not sin against thee."* The Holy Spirit will cause you to remember verses as you witness, to give you hope, to help you flee temptation, and to provide direction in times of decision.

Journaling

Writing or journaling has the power to help you see God's hand at work in your life and circumstances. As you read the Bible, you'll be encouraged, convicted, moved, blessed, and challenged. Use this journal to record how God is working in your heart and mind through His Word. You may find that journaling helps bring healing from the past or gives you clarity for the future, but it ultimately should be a record of the goodness of God.

The Application

Application is the goal of our devotional time. Ask yourself, "How can what I read make me more like Christ?" "How can I apply this truth to my life today?" Francis Bacon wisely stated, "It is not what men eat but what they digest that makes them strong; not what we gain but what we save that makes us rich; not what we read but what we remember that makes us learned; not what we preach but what we practice that makes us Christians."

The Bible is powerful and practical, but it must be applied to and lived out in our daily lives. God desires that we put the truths we've learned into practice through obedience to His Word. When we refuse to obey the Scriptures, we are only hurting ourselves.

> *But be ye doers of the word, and not hearers only, deceiving your own selves.*—JAMES 1:22

> *I thought on my ways, and turned my feet unto thy testimonies. I made haste, and delayed not to keep thy commandments.* —PSALM 119:59–60

A.W. Tozer said, "Unused truth becomes as useless as an unused muscle."

God's Word is the only way to satisfy a hungry soul. When you come before Him with a pure heart, your utmost attention, a surrendered will, and an eagerness to feast on truth, it is then that your soul will most certainly be fed.

> *This Book is the mind of God, the state of man, the way of salvation, the doom of sinners, and the happiness of believers. Its doctrines are holy, its precepts are binding; its histories are true, and its decisions are immutable. Read it to be wise, believe it to be safe, practice it to be holy. It contains light to direct you, food to support you, and comfort to cheer you. It is the traveler's map, the pilgrim's staff, the pilot's compass, the soldier's sword, and the Christian's character. Here paradise is restored, Heaven opened, and the gates of hell disclosed. Christ is its grand subject, our good its design, and the glory of God its end. It should fill the memory, rule the heart, and guide the feet. Read it slowly, frequently, prayerfully. It is a mine of wealth, a paradise of glory, and a river of pleasure. Follow its precepts and it will lead you to Calvary, to the empty tomb, to a resurrected life in Christ; yes, to glory itself, for eternity.*—AUTHOR UNKNOWN

TWO

Develop Your Prayer Life

Far too many Christian women have never discovered the incredible resources available through a meaningful prayer life. Prayer should never be our last resort but our first resource. Yet, statistics say that prayer is the most often talked about and the least practiced discipline in the Christian life. Whether your day to day life is struggling or soaring, we all must have hearts that are willing to develop and deepen our communication with the Lord. We need to share our hearts with Him and seek His resources to meet our needs

Reasons to Pray

God does incredible works on our behalf simply through prayer. As you read through these, I hope they will encourage you as you work to develop your prayer life.

Prayer Increases Faith

Dr. Howard Hendricks, a Christian educator, was asked how to teach children to have faith. His answer: *Instruct them to keep a prayer list!* As we see God answer prayer, it increases our faith in His power and in His care to hear our prayers. This benefit of prayer is so significant that in the prayer pages beginning on page 53, I've included a column for you to record when God answers specific prayers on your list.

Prayer Releases Burdens

Prayer also allows us to release our burdens. All of us carry burdens whether or not we talk about them, and prayer gives us the opportunity to unload our cares on the Lord. It is so much better to go to the Lord instead of unloading on our husbands or, worse yet, another woman! God doesn't repeat what I tell Him; He does not judge what I say; and He understands everything.

Ladies sometimes come to me for counsel, and early in our conversation they sometimes say, "You just don't understand." I tell them they're probably right, but I know Someone who does. The Bible says in Psalm 147:5, *"Great is our Lord, and of great power: his understanding is infinite."* What a comforting verse! Not only does the Lord understand, but He has the power to do something about the burden.

The longer we hold onto our burdens, the heavier they become to our hearts. God never intended for us to carry our life's burdens alone. First Peter 5:7 says, *"Casting all your care upon him; for he careth for you."* God wants to bear our load. He designed us to need His help in carrying the weight that life puts on our shoulders. John Baillie said, "Give me a stout heart to bear my own burdens. Give me a willing heart to bear the burdens of others. Give me a believing heart to cast all burdens upon Thee, O Lord."

What burdens are you carrying today? Are you tired of hauling them around? Are they becoming heavier and heavier to your heart? Friend, I encourage you to cast your cares upon Him. You weren't meant to bear your burdens alone, and God is eager to carry your load. He is waiting to hear from you.

Prayer Reminds Us of God's Nearness

Prayer teaches us that God is always near. We are the ones who shy away from God. It's not the other way around! Hebrews 10:22 tells us, *"Let us draw near with a true heart in full assurance of faith, having our hearts sprinkled from an evil conscience, and our bodies washed with pure water."* Oswald Chambers said, "The purpose of prayer is to reveal the presence of God equally present all the time in every condition." And Psalm 145:18 promises, *"The LORD is nigh unto all them that call upon him, to all that call upon him in truth."*

Often, we feel like we are drowning under the burdens and pressures of life, when all we have to do is reach out to the Lord. He is close by, waiting to help, ready to strengthen us, yet we just stand there alone. The question is not, "How close is God?" The question is, "Will you reach out to Him?" He is as near to you as He has always been. Why not reach out to Him right now, seek His help, and cast yourself upon Him in full and complete dependence?

Prayer Provides Power

There is power in prayer—not because of what we pray, but because God is powerful. Edwin Harvey said, "A day without prayer is a day without blessing, and a life without prayer is a life without power."

God has the power to transform you, your circumstances, your husband, and your marriage. On the other hand, Satan wants to destroy your marriage and the only way you can truly defeat him is through prayer. Guy King observed, "No one is a firmer believer in the power of prayer than the devil; not that he practices it, but he suffers from it."

Don't settle for a life lived in your own strength and effort. Ask God for His power, depend on it for a fruitful Christian life, and give Him the glory as He works on your behalf. James 5:16 promises us, *"The effectual fervent prayer of a righteous man availeth much."*

Prayer Changes Our Lives

Prayer changes us! That truth gives us another reason to go before the throne of God.

Usually, our perspective in prayer is not that we need to change, but something or someone else needs to change. Sometimes our prayers are focused more on altering someone else than on allowing the Holy Spirit to transform us. Our prayer should always be, "Lord, I am standing in the need of prayer...change me."

I pray that these "reasons" to pray have challenged you to have a right perspective in your Christian walk—a prayer perspective. May your sincere desire be to bring your heart to God consistently in prayer. As we serve the Lord, prayer will keep our hearts tender, our lives growing, and our relationship with the Lord strong.

Praying for Yourself

Nothing can make a difference in your life more than prayer. But sometimes we wonder why we are not getting our prayers answered. Sometimes the reason is simply that God hasn't answered *yet*. But sometimes the reason is that personal sin is clogging communication with Heaven. When you go before the Lord, you want nothing to hinder your communication with Him. We have an all-knowing Father who is willing and ready to forgive and cleanse us, yet we try to ignore or cover sin rather than confess and forsake it.

> *Search me, O God, and know my heart: try me, and know my thoughts: And see if there be any wicked way in me, and lead me in the way everlasting.*—PSALM 139:23–24

If we confess our sins, he is faithful and just to forgive us our sins, and to cleanse us from all unrighteousness. —1 JOHN 1:9

The first is an invitation to the Holy Spirit to search every corner of your life, and the second is a reminder of God's guaranteed forgiveness. Begin your prayer time by asking the Lord to search your heart, because a clean heart gives you freedom to pour out your requests to Him.

Praying for Your Husband

I'm always blessed when readers of *It's a Wonderful Life* mention a specific way the book had an impact on their lives. One of the most frequently mentioned sections of that book is the list I included of ways to specifically pray for your husband.

Sometimes when we pray for others, we find ourselves repeating the same lines: "And bless my husband today...." Over the years, I have been helped in collecting specific ways to pray for my husband. Your list may look different than the one below, but hopefully this will give you a start and some ideas.

You can pray:

- That he will be Spirit filled
- That he will have a strong walk with the Lord
- That he will have a productive day
- That God will bless his appointments
- That he will be able to handle the stress of the day
- That God will give him wisdom in counseling
- That he would have a sense of fulfillment
- That he would have sufficient study time
- That God will strengthen him in his burdens
- That God will protect him from temptation
- That God will give protection from anyone wanting to hurt him
- That God will protect his reputation
- That he will be healthy—keep him well

- That God will heal him if he is sick
- For his responsibilities
- For his priorities
- That he will be a good leader
- For those whom he leads
- For his role as a father
- For safety as he travels
- For refreshment as he travels
- For no delays as he travels
- That God will make him strong where he is weak
- That God will give him the courage to make right choices
- That he will be encouraged
- For his vision
- That God will direct his path
- That he will be fruitful
- For his friends
- For safety from any danger
- That he would maintain balance in all his roles
- For sermons he is preparing
- That God will safeguard his heart
- That he will continue to love righteousness and hate wickedness
- That he will have self-control
- That he will have peace and joy
- That God will give him wisdom in disciplining the children
- That he will recognize the lies of the enemy

Imagine the profound impact you could have on your husband's life and ministry if you would bring these requests before the Lord on a regular basis. Imagine how your heart might fill with a deeper love for God and for him! You can also pray for your husband from head to toe as Sylvia Gunter recommends in her book, *Prayer Portions*.

His head—That he may lead you

His mind—That he may know Christ

His eyes—That he may see from God's perspective and be aware of spiritual danger

His ears—That he may hear God's words with his heart

His nose—That he will be a refreshing fragrance

His mouth—That he would have boldness in speaking of Christ and wisdom to keep the door of his lips

His bones—That he would be healthy

His heart—That he would obey with his whole heart

His arms—That God would be his arm every morning—Isaiah 33:2

His hands—That he will bless God as long as he lives—Psalm 63:4

His legs—That he will walk by faith

His feet—That God will direct his steps[1]

Praying Effectively

A sure way to receive specific answers from the Lord is to pray specific prayers. It's important to go before the Lord with sincerity, but a useful way to help organize your requests is to maintain a prayer list—you can't possibly remember all of your needs and the needs of others without keeping record. Your prayer list will be one of the most helpful tools in your communion with the Heavenly Father. (You can use the blank Prayer List in the back of this journal.)

There are also two acrostics that may help you communicate with the Lord more effectively—PRAYER and ACTS:

P — **Praise.** Praise the Lord for His attributes and thank Him for His goodness.

R — **Repent.** Confess all known sin. Keep short accounts with God.

A — **Ask.** Take requests to God.

---

1.   Sylvia Gunter, *Prayer Portions*, (Murphy, OR: Castle Peak Editions, 1991).

Y — Yield. Yield to the Lord and to His Word.

E — Everyone. Then pray for others: family, missionaries, pastors' wives, friends.

R — Read God's Word. Conclude your time of prayer by listening to God through His Word.

Another acrostic that works well as a prayer pattern is ACTS:

A — Adoration

C — Confession

T — Thanksgiving

S — Supplication

Don't go before the Lord with requests without first telling Him how good He is and don't expect Him to hear those same requests when you have a heart full of unconfessed sin. Praise, confession, and sincerity are the keys to a successful prayer life.

Prayer is God's invitation to fellowship with Him, worship Him, and unburden our souls to Him. He listens, cares, and answers. No one would receive an invitation like this and ignore it or find something else to do. But every day, sometimes without even realizing it, we make the choice to accept or reject the invitation. Instead of spending time in prayer, we choose to let our minds wander and worry. Instead of talking to the Lord, we talk to a friend. Instead of reaching up to take the hand of the Father, we try to do it all on our own.

Prayer is a gift, an opportunity, a joy. It is also a decision that we must make every day of our lives. And when we choose to pray, it is a wonderful life!

THREE

Strengthen Your Relationships

This is my commandment, That ye love one another, as I have loved you. Greater love hath no man than this, that a man lay down his life for his friends. Ye are my friends, if ye do whatsoever I command you. Henceforth I call you not servants; for the servant knoweth not what his lord doeth: but I have called you friends; for all things that I have heard of my Father I have made known unto you.—JOHN 15:12–15

A man that hath friends must shew himself friendly: and there is a friend that sticketh closer than a brother.—PROVERBS 18:24

Life is too short and at times too difficult to live alone. That is why God gave us the gift of earthly relationships. We must daily be working at developing and cultivating connections that will draw us closer to Him.

A Wonderful Purpose

While our vertical relationship with the Father is most important, He has lovingly given us human relationships for a specific purpose.

> *Two are better than one; because they have a good reward for their labour. For if they fall, the one will lift up his fellow: but woe to him that is alone when he falleth; for he hath not another to help him up.*—ECCLESIASTES 4:9–10

Bearing Burdens

A burden is defined as "the care we carry in our heart." Whether we are young or old, a new or mature Christian, everyone carries a burden. People don't have the ability to take away burdens—only God can do that. Friends, however, are prime candidates to help strengthen, love, and encourage in a time of need. Phillip Brooks said, "The truest help we can render an afflicted man is not to take his burden from him, but to call out his best strength that he may be able to bear the burden." You can "strengthen" someone by praying for them and by sharing scripture.

Accountability

God has given us friendships for bearing burdens but also for accountability.

The story is told of early African converts who were sincere and consistent in their private devotions. Each one reportedly had a separate spot in a thicket where he would pour out his heart to God. Over time, the paths to these places became well worn. As a result, if one of these believers began to neglect his prayer time, it was soon apparent to the others. They would kindly remind the negligent one, "Brother, the grass grows on your path."

Have you given someone in your life the liberty to say, "The grass is growing on your path"? Be accountable in your walk with God. Ask a friend or your spouse to hold you accountable in your devotions. Allow this person to ask questions, wake you up in the morning, listen to memorized verses, or do whatever it takes to encourage you in building a relationship with God.

A Wonderful Friend

The Bible often talks about friendship. And it doesn't talk so much about *having* friends as it does about *being* a good friend. Here are a few marks of a good friend that may be helpful to you:

1. Good friends sharpen each other. Proverbs 27:17 teaches us that *"iron sharpeneth iron."* A godly friend will "sharpen" you and vice versa. Good friends will make you a better person. Healthy relationships challenge us to grow in wisdom and knowledge by offering a different perspective or difference of opinion.

2. Good friends stick around. Godly friends love each other. But Proverbs 17:17 teaches that friends love at **all times**—especially in adversity. The old saying is true, "Prosperity begets friendship; adversity reveals them." Do you have the kind of friendship who is strong and built upon the bond you share in Christ? If you want to have strong relationships that last, ask God to first make you a consistent friend.

3. Good friends make memories. Engaging in activity and fellowship with other believers is a fun way to strengthen friendships. Road trips, hiking, joining a book club, taking a painting class, or simply enjoying a bowl of ice cream are great ways to make memories. Proverbs 17:22 says, *"A merry heart doeth good like a medicine...."* So, laugh, have a good time, and enjoy fellowship with other Christians.

4. Godly friends rejoice for one another. A Swedish proverb states, "Friendship doubles our joy and divides our grief." Godly friends rejoice in our blessings and sorrow in our disappointments. Strong friendships have no room for jealousy, comparison, or envy.

5. Godly friends forgive. We are all born sinners, so even friends will eventually hurt each other—and it's usually unintentionally. Yet, when God is present in a relationship, there can always be peace. Godly friends resolve tension and quickly forgive. Proverbs 22:24 teaches that we should avoid friendship with an angry person—pray and ask God for a heart that is gracious and forgiving.

6. Good friends encourage. Proverbs 15:23 says, *"A man hath joy by the answer of his mouth: and a word spoken in due season, how good is it!"* And Proverbs 12:25 teaches, *"Heaviness in the heart of man maketh it stoop: but a good word maketh it glad."*

Encouragement goes straight to the heart. In fact, the word itself comes from a combination of the prefix *en* which means "to put into" and the Latin word *cor* which means "heart." We literally have the ability to pour hope, strength, and spiritual motivation into the heart of another Christian. That's a pretty awesome privilege! Being an encouragement is not hard! It's as easy as talking to someone or writing a kind note!

God has given you His Word full of encouraging truth. As you read and are encouraged, think of ways you can show the love of Christ and edify someone in your life; whether that be your spouse, your neighbor, a sibling, close friend, or acquaintance.

7. Godly friends spark the truth in each other. Proverbs 27:6 says, *"Faithful are the wounds of a friend...."* Godly friends are not afraid to "speak the truth in love" (see Ephesians 4:15) to one another. In fact, they *want* to hear the truth. Good friends understand that we may not always see our own shortcomings, but they rejoice in knowing that God has given them "another set of spiritual eyes" to help guide, guard, and protect. Beyond that, godly friends rejoice in truth. They seek truth together. They talk about truth. They encourage each other with truth. Truth is the common bond of their hearts—a love for God's Word and a love for communicating His truth to others.

The greatest attribute of a good friend is sacrifice. John 15:13 says that: *"Greater love hath no man than this, that **a man lay down his life for his friends**."* You may not be called upon to literally give your life for anybody. You may, however, be called to sacrifice your wants, your needs, or your time, to give them the first turn and the last cookie and anything else that is hard to give. There is no greater love on earth than the love of sacrifice! There is no greater friend than a friend who loves like Jesus loves and the way we become that friend is by spending time with Him daily in His Word. It's been said that you become who you hang out with. And that is awesome news to the person who spends time with Jesus!

Remember, no one is above the need for daily exhortation and encouragement from being around other Christians. While fun and encouragement are needed, the foundational purpose for strengthening your earthly relationships is to point one another to Jesus Christ. Let's strengthen each other for the glory of God!

FOUR

Trust God's Goodness

As wonderful as it is to know and follow the Lord as we grow in our relationship with Him, see Him answer our prayers, and develop godly friendships, there are seasons when we are tempted to think following Christ is *not* a wonderful life—those times when we encounter trials and difficulty.

The truth is, trials are common to all people—those who know the Lord and those who don't. We who know the Lord, however, have the presence of God with us and grace from God to not just survive the trials, but to grow through them.

We all would choose sunshine over showers, but just imagine what our world would be like if it never rained again! Franklin Elmer described a place of no rain located in Northern Chile. He wrote, "Morning after morning the sun rises brilliantly over the tall mountains to the east; each noon it shines brightly down from overhead; evening brings a picturesque sunset. Although storms are often seen raging high in the mountains, and heavy fog banks are observed far out over the sea, the sun continues to shine on this favored and protected strip of land. One would imagine this area to be an earthly paradise, but it is not. Instead, it is a sterile and desolate desert! There are no streams of water, and nothing grows there." Nothing will grow in a life free of trials. And a life without "rain" does not exist.

Beloved, think it not strange concerning the fiery trial which is to try you, as though some strange thing happened unto you:
—1 PETER 4:12

Trials are burdensome. Even though we know we will experience trials, it is not always easy to accept them. They can be difficult and painful to bear. We will often ask God to remove the burden, and, though God may not always take it away, He will develop in us stronger muscle for the load. Corrie Ten Boom said, "If God sends us on stony paths, He provides strong shoes."

The good news is that trials are temporary and we can rejoice in the fact that trials don't last forever.

For I reckon that the sufferings of this present time are not worthy to be compared with the glory which shall be revealed in us.—ROMANS 8:18

The suffering we temporarily experience on this earth is not even worthy to be compared to what God has in store for us in Heaven. What a comforting promise to claim for our lives! This life is a temporal life, so keep your heart focused on eternity. The longest any trial could last is the duration of a lifetime, which in comparison to eternity, is almost nothing. Live with eternity in mind.

There hath no temptation taken you but such as is common to man: but God is faithful, who will not suffer you to be

tempted above that ye are able; but will with the temptation also make a way to escape, that ye may be able to bear it.
—1 Corinthians 10:13

Remember: whenever there is the presence of trials, there is the presence of God. Isaiah 43:2 promises, *"When thou passest through the waters, I will be with thee; and through the rivers, they shall not overflow thee: when thou walkest through the fire, thou shalt not be burned; neither shall the flame kindle upon thee."*

God is our refuge and strength, a very present help in trouble.
—Psalm 46:1

The Purpose of Trials

Your understanding of God's purpose in testing will determine your ability to withstand the turmoil and uproar that takes place during that testing. Understanding God's purposes will help you to find peace and stability when you are feeling that your world is turned upside down. Trials do have a purpose!

Trials are prescribed to meet our needs. First Peter 1:6 says, *"Wherein ye greatly rejoice, though now for a season, if need be, ye are in heaviness through manifold temptations."* "If need be" indicates that God knows there will be periods of life in which we need to experience testing. Be comforted by the truth that our Father knows each of our needs better than we know our own. He knows when we need a trial and when we need to be shaken up to avoid spiritual death. We pray that you wouldn't have to experience a trial—unless it is needed for the sake of your spiritual life. If that is the case, then we pray that you will learn the lessons God has in store for you as a result of this time.

Trials are the pathway back to God. Often, when things are going well, we have a propensity to go our own way, spend less time on our knees, and seek the Lord with less than our whole hearts. Trials are often designed for the purpose of bringing us back to God.

> *Before I was afflicted I went astray: but now have I kept thy word.*—PSALM 119:67.

He wants to perfect you, not pamper you. He wants you to grow spiritually!

> *And he said unto me, My grace is sufficient for thee: for my strength is made perfect in weakness. Most gladly therefore will I rather glory in my infirmities, that the power of Christ may rest upon me.*—2 CORINTHIANS 12:9

Trials purify us. It is God's desire that we would be pure vessels, fit for the Master's use. There are times in life when God must not only clean us, but He must mold, bend, hammer, and shape us. These times are difficult to experience, but they are necessary for our purification. A goldsmith would never deliberately waste precious ore. Instead, he would put it into the furnace long enough to remove the cheap impurities. He would pour it out and make from it a beautiful article of value.

> *For they verily for a few days chastened us after their own pleasure; but he for our profit, that we might be partakers of his holiness.*—HEBREWS 12:10

> *Take away the dross from the silver, and there shall come forth a vessel for the finer.*—PROVERBS 25:4

Trials teach us to personify Christ. Just as the goldsmith keeps the metal in the furnace until he can see his reflection, so our Lord keeps us in the furnace of suffering until we reflect the glory and beauty of Jesus Christ. Responding to times of difficulty in a Christ-like manner is a great testimony to unsaved people who watch you. As we allow God's grace to work in our hearts, we can also encourage fellow Christians by our faithfulness and example.

Trials point others to God. Many biblical examples prove this principle. The gospel was spread because of the trial that Paul experienced in the Philippian jail. And because of the persecution of the three Hebrew children, Nebuchadnezzar made a decree that he would destroy those who said anything against the God of Shadrach, Meshach, and Abednego. Is your response to trials one that can point others to the Saviour? God will point all men to Himself. Are you an instrument that He can use to accomplish that purpose?

Trials display the power of God in our lives. I don't know about you, but I need and want God's power in my life! One way to experience God's power is through the presence of trials. God's power is greater than our emotions and our weaknesses, and it is displayed as we allow Him to work in our lives during times of suffering.

> *And lest I should be exalted above measure through the abundance of the revelations, there was given to me a thorn in the flesh, the messenger of Satan to buffet me, lest I should be exalted above measure. For this thing I besought the Lord thrice, that it might depart from me. And he said unto me, My grace is sufficient for thee: for my strength is made perfect in weakness. Most gladly therefore will I rather glory in my infirmities, that the power of Christ may rest upon me. Therefore I take pleasure in infirmities, in reproaches, in necessities, in persecutions, in distresses for Christ's sake: for when I am weak, then am I strong.*—2 CORINTHIANS 12:7–10

Responding to Trials

Every trial gives us the opportunity to learn something wonderful about our Saviour. During one trial, we might learn of His grace. The next testing may encourage us with a new awareness of His strength. And the following trial may remind us of His promises and His comfort. We can also learn to experience and exhibit the fruit of the Spirit: love, joy, peace, longsuffering, gentleness, goodness, faith, meekness, and temperance. Listening and learning rather than being defensive and close-minded is the best way to deal with a difficult situation. How can we respond to a trial in a way that we might grow through it?

Respond to the trial with God's perspective. Does your trial reveal any areas of your life that need change? If so, confess the sin and get rid of the hindrances. Perhaps you are being criticized. Consider the accuracy of the criticism. Is there any part that is true? What can you change for God's glory? Trials may come into your life because of sin, irresponsible behavior, or a bad decision—immediately confess these to God. After your confession, take the appropriate steps to resolve it. If, to your knowledge, you have done nothing to bring the trial upon yourself, assume it is from God's loving hand for your benefit and His glory.

Stay faithful. God requires us to be faithful even during tough times. Hebrews 12:1 says, *"Wherefore seeing we also are compassed about with so great a cloud of witnesses, let us lay aside every weight, and the sin which doth so easily beset us, and let us run with patience the race that is set before us."* That means: Don't give out. Don't give in. Don't give up. Don't quit. Don't jump off the Potter's wheel before the Potter is finished molding you into a usable vessel! Finish your course so you can say as Paul did in 2 Timothy 4:7, *"I have fought a good fight, I have finished my course, I have kept the faith."*

Pray. Take your trials and burdens to the Lord in prayer; give Him the hurt that is in your heart. You may have different verses of hymns that come to mind during different stages, occasions, or circumstances in your life. Meditate on those verses and songs and be encouraged at how God uses that to comfort you.

Is any among you afflicted? let him pray. Is any merry? let him sing psalms.—JAMES 5:13

Here are a few verses that might be helpful to you:

Hold up my goings in thy paths, that my footsteps slip not. I have called upon thee, for thou wilt hear me, O God: incline thine ear unto me, and hear my speech. Shew thy marvellous lovingkindness, O thou that savest by thy right hand them which put their trust in thee from those that rise up against them. Keep me as the apple of the eye, hide me under the shadow of thy wings,—PSALM 17:5–8

My voice shalt thou hear in the morning, O LORD; in the morning will I direct my prayer unto thee, and will look up.—PSALM 5:3

Cast thy burden upon the LORD, and he shall sustain thee: he shall never suffer the righteous to be moved.—PSALM 55:22

Therefore, my beloved brethren, be ye stedfast, unmoveable, always abounding in the work of the Lord, forasmuch as ye know that your labour is not in vain in the Lord.—1 CORINTHIANS 15:58

Not that I speak in respect of want: for I have learned, in whatsoever state I am, therewith to be content.—PHILIPPIANS 4:11

Only take heed to thyself, and keep thy soul diligently, lest thou forget the things which thine eyes have seen, and lest they depart from thy heart all the days of thy life: but teach them thy sons, and thy sons' sons;—DEUTERONOMY 4:9

I have glorified thee on the earth: I have finished the work which thou gavest me to do.—JOHN 17:4

I have fought a good fight, I have finished my course, I have kept the faith:—2 TIMOTHY 4:7

Rejoice. James 1:2 says, *"My brethren, count it all joy when ye fall into divers temptations."* Unlike happiness, which is dependent upon circumstances, joy is a condition of the heart that we can possess no matter what we are going through. Joy is a choice! We can choose to pout and feel sorry for ourselves, or we can rest in knowing that God has a purpose for this trial and He is working it out for His good. When things are going well, we talk about how good God is, and we rejoice in the great things He has done. But what about when the pressures come, the burdens are heavy, and the trials are tough; do we still rejoice in the Lord? Philippians 4:4 tells us, *"Rejoice in the Lord alway: and again I say, Rejoice."*

What does it mean to "rejoice in the Lord"? It means that, even in the midst of pain, we rejoice in the never-changing character of our God. And it also means that we rejoice in what God's presence means in our suffering. For instance, because of verses like Psalm 5:11, I can rejoice in the fact that the Lord will defend me from those who are against me: *"But let all those that put their trust in thee rejoice: let them ever shout for joy, because thou defendest them: let them also that love thy name be joyful in thee."* God promises to meet us when we rejoice in Him. Isaiah 64:5 says, *"Thou meetest him that rejoiceth and worketh righteousness, those that remember thee in thy ways: behold, thou art wroth; for we have sinned: in those is continuance, and we shall be saved."* God also promises that His joy will sustain us. Nehemiah 8:10 tells us, *"...the joy of the LORD is your strength."* Do you need strength during your trial? Learn to find your joy in the Lord!

Trust. Why is it that we can easily trust humans but fail to trust the Lord completely when life has a little turmoil? Sometimes it is hard to trust the Lord through difficult circumstances because we want our will or our outcome. Trust is allowing God to control the circumstances. Fear hinders us from trusting God, because we fret over what might happen or how things will turn out. Remember, God never makes a mistake; He never forgets about us; He never forsakes us; and He will never betray us! We don't have to fear the future if we are trusting the heart of God.

For I know the thoughts that I think toward you, saith the LORD, thoughts of peace, and not of evil, to give you an expected end.
—JEREMIAH 29:11

And we know that all things work together for good to them that love God, to them who are the called according to his purpose.
—ROMANS 8:28

Casting all your care upon him; for he careth for you.
—1 PETER 5:7

Wherefore let them that suffer according to the will of God commit the keeping of their souls to him in well doing, as unto a faithful Creator.—1 PETER 4:19

Thou wilt keep him in perfect peace, whose mind is stayed on thee: because he trusteth in thee.—ISAIAH 26:3

Don't become bitter. Trials should make you better, not bitter! A bitter spirit is extremely destructive. It drives wedges between friends, co-laborers, husbands and wives, brothers and sisters, and parents and children. Be ready to rebuild broken relationships that may come as a part of a trial. Always be sensitive to the Spirit's leading toward healing a relationship.

Focus on the Lord. When suffering or trials come along, there is a tendency to focus on the pain and the problems. My little brother was playing in the garage when he was about five-years-old. He wanted to cut a piece of string, but he couldn't find any scissors. So he used a hatchet that was nearby! He missed the string and cut the tips of two fingers! He came running into the house holding his hand. When I saw his two fingers, I wanted to scream, cry, or hide, but my mom told me I had to keep his mind off of his hand. So all the way to the doctor I talked to him about fishing and baseball in an effort to keep his focus away from his pain.

When you are in pain, don't focus on it! Don't examine the wound and rehearse the injury. Focus on God! God must be your focal point when the pain becomes intense. He will provide the encouragement, motivation, and strength you need to make it through. Peter learned this same principle when he walked with Jesus on the water. He was able to stay above the circumstances when he kept his focus on Jesus.

The Prize after the Trial

God brings great blessings in our lives through trials.

> *But rejoice, inasmuch as ye are partakers of Christ's sufferings; that, when his glory shall be revealed, ye may be glad also with exceeding joy.*—1 PETER 4:13

We are useful to God. An instrument is useful only if it's in the right shape. A dull ax or a bent screwdriver needs attention, and so do we, if we are dull or bent in our spiritual lives. A good blacksmith keeps his tools in shape and so does God. He desires that you come out of your trial better than you entered in. This is certainly easier said than done, but when God places you in a trial, be thankful. It means He thinks you are still worth reshaping!

> *If a man therefore purge himself from these, he shall be a vessel unto honour, sanctified, and meet for the master's use, and prepared unto every good work.*—2 TIMOTHY 2:21

We learn patience. Even though we don't always like the process, the Bible tells us that trials produce patience.

> *Knowing this, that the trying of your faith worketh patience. But let patience have her perfect work, that ye may be perfect and entire, wanting nothing.*—JAMES 1:3–4

We experience peace. God promises His peace as a result of suffering. And God's peace is a peace that passes all understanding!

*Be careful for nothing; but in every thing by prayer and supplication with thanksgiving let your requests be made known unto God. And the peace of God, which passeth all understanding, shall keep your hearts and minds through Christ Jesus.—*PHILIPPIANS 4:6–7

God has not promised skies always blue,
Flower-strewn pathways all our life through;
God has not promised sun without rain,
Joy without sorrow, peace without pain.
But God has promised strength for the day,
Rest for the labor, light for the way;
Grace for the trials, help from above,
Unfailing sympathy, undying love.
—SOURCE UNKNOWN

Ask the Lord today to give you a new perspective on trials and testing and determine to be a Christian who grows through whatever circumstances the Lord allows in your life. And as you go through trials and seek the Lord's strength in those moments, remember to record in this journal how God brought you through the difficulty and what you are learning—you'll be a better Christian for it.

FIVE

Record the Journey

*"It's hard for me to keep a diary because it seems to me that I—
nor anyone else for that matter—would ever be interested in the
secrets of a thirteen-year-old school girl."*—ANNE FRANK, 1942

When thirteen-year-old Anne Frank scribbled those words in the upstairs attic where she and her family were hiding from the Nazis, she could have had no idea that because of her diary, she would become a symbol for Jews who lost their lives during World War II.

We often see our lives—and especially the individual days that comprise them—as insignificant. Yet, each day—and especially what God does in our hearts through His Word—matters.

Part two of this journal is really the heart of the journal because it encourages you to record your journey with the Lord.

Now, I'll be the first to admit that our journals will probably never be turned into books or movies, but they will leave a legacy for those who follow behind us. Journals also serve as personal memorials in our own lives. They often provide encouragement in times of uncertainty and joy in times of reminiscing as we meditate on the work and goodness of God in our lives.

If there is one area of my life that I regret at this point, it is that I did not journal more consistently and take more pictures in years past. I used to say, "I will never forget that," and then I did! It seems impossible to remember all the events of your life accurately, so be sure to record significant events and important seasons of growth.

Part of our problem is that we rarely see the significance of what God is doing in the moment. Just as Anne Frank thought the little things of her life didn't matter, we assume that the "small" answers to prayer, the "little" blessings, and the "coincidental" verses of encouragement we find in God's Word are insignificant. But the "small stuff" is everything—it is what our stories are made of. No blessing from God or special event allowed by Him is too small to record for ourselves and for those who come after us.

In the following pages, you'll be prompted during your time with the Lord each day to record individual aspects of the wonderful life God is putting together for you.

On the opposite page is a sample of the pages from your daily pages. Let's walk through it together:

Today's date—While I encourage you to journal every day, I've left this blank for you so you never have to skip pages in this journal if you miss a day. Sometimes starting a new habit takes time, so be patient with yourself if you miss, and come back the next day.

Passage I read—You may want to simply write the reference of what you read in this spot, or you may want to write out a specific verse that spoke to you. However you use it, this section can record your journey through God's Word.

TODAY'S A
WONDERFUL DAY

TODAY'S DATE _____ / _____ / _____

notes

passage I read:

_____
_____
_____
_____
_____
_____
_____

truths for my day:

_____
_____
_____
_____
_____
_____

today I'm thankful for:

_____
_____
_____
_____

This is the day which the Lord hath made; we will rejoice and be glad in it.—Psalm 118:24

Truths for my day—Remember, the goal of Bible reading is not knowledge, but application. Use this section to jot down a simple thought of how you can apply what you have read on a given day. Some days it may be a single sentence, and some days it may be a more developed truth as you record how it relates to specific circumstances in your life. There is no right or wrong way to do it. Just use this as a prompt to help apply God's truth to your day.

Today I am thankful for—If you're like me, you find it easier to see areas you need to grow in your life than to remember the good work that God is already doing. This section will remind you to "Rejoice in the Lord" (Philippians 4:4) as you write down something for which you are thankful. You may write something you are thankful for about God Himself, or you may record an answer to prayer, or simply take a moment to thank the Lord for one of the many good gifts He gives to us every day. Expressing gratitude for God's goodness in your life will also help your perspective on days that don't feel so wonderful.

Notes—This section is intentionally left blank so you can use it however best suits you. If you are creative and artistic, you may decide to draw here or to create beautiful lettering from one of the verses in your quiet time. If you're easily distracted (like me), you may use this to record those persistent little to-dos that come to mind while you're trying to spend time with the Lord. It may be a spot to write down someone else who God places on your heart to write a note to. Or it may be a good place to write daily goals or special memories.

I pray that the process of using these pages will be an encouragement to you and that as you look back over what you have written some months down the road, you'll see God's hand working in the small details, in the good days and bad, to create a beautiful big picture—a truly wonderful life.

SIX
Bible Reading Schedules

Second Timothy 3:16 describes the profit that God's Word brings to our lives: *"All scripture is given by inspiration of God, and is profitable for doctrine, for reproof, for correction, for instruction in righteousness."*

Did you catch the four provisions of the Scriptures?

Doctrine—it teaches us the truth.

Reproof—it convicts us when we are wrong.

Correction—it tells us how to realign our lives to the truth.

Instruction—it provides directions to live the truth and enjoy its benefits.

We *need* these provisions—doctrine, reproof, correction, and instruction—in our lives on a daily basis. Thus, we need God's Word. The Bible reading schedules on the following pages are available to help guide you in a systematic reading of God's Word.

one-year schedule

January

Day	Old Testament	New Testament	✔
1	Gen. 1–3	Matt. 1	☐
2	Gen. 4–6	Matt. 2	☐
3	Gen. 7–9	Matt. 3	☐
4	Gen. 10–12	Matt. 4	☐
5	Gen. 13–15	Matt. 5:1–26	☐
6	Gen. 16–17	Matt. 5:27–48	☐
7	Gen. 18–19	Matt. 6:1–18	☐
8	Gen. 20–22	Matt. 6:19–34	☐
9	Gen. 23–24	Matt. 7	☐
10	Gen. 25–26	Matt. 8:1–17	☐
11	Gen. 27–28	Matt. 8:18–34	☐
12	Gen. 29–30	Matt. 9:1–17	☐
13	Gen. 31–32	Matt. 9:18–38	☐
14	Gen. 33–35	Matt. 10:1–20	☐
15	Gen. 36–38	Matt. 10:21–42	☐
16	Gen. 39–40	Matt. 11	☐
17	Gen. 41–42	Matt. 12:1–23	☐
18	Gen. 43–45	Matt. 12:24–50	☐
19	Gen. 46–48	Matt. 13:1–30	☐
20	Gen. 49–50	Matt. 13:31–58	☐
21	Ex. 1–3	Matt. 14:1–21	☐
22	Ex. 4–6	Matt. 14:22–36	☐
23	Ex. 7–8	Matt. 15:1–20	☐
24	Ex. 9–11	Matt. 15:21–39	☐
25	Ex. 12–13	Matt. 16	☐
26	Ex. 14–15	Matt. 17	☐
27	Ex. 16–18	Matt. 18:1–20	☐
28	Ex. 19–20	Matt. 18:21–35	☐
29	Ex. 21–22	Matt. 19	☐
30	Ex. 23–24	Matt. 20:1–16	☐
31	Ex. 25–26	Matt. 20:17–34	☐

February

Day	Old Testament	New Testament	✔
1	Ex. 27–28	Matt. 21:1–22	☐
2	Ex. 29–30	Matt. 21:23–46	☐
3	Ex. 31–33	Matt. 22:1–22	☐
4	Ex. 34–35	Matt. 22:23–46	☐
5	Ex. 36–38	Matt. 23:1–22	☐
6	Ex. 39–40	Matt. 23:23–39	☐
7	Lev. 1–3	Matt. 24:1–28	☐
8	Lev. 4–5	Matt. 24:29–51	☐
9	Lev. 6–7	Matt. 25:1–30	☐
10	Lev. 8–10	Matt. 25:31–46	☐
11	Lev. 11–12	Matt. 26:1–25	☐
12	Lev. 13	Matt. 26:26–50	☐
13	Lev. 14	Matt. 26:51–75	☐
14	Lev. 15–16	Matt. 27:1–26	☐
15	Lev. 17–18	Matt. 27:27–50	☐
16	Lev. 19–20	Matt. 27:51–66	☐
17	Lev. 21–22	Matt. 28	☐
18	Lev. 23–24	Mark 1:1–22	☐
19	Lev. 25	Mark 1:23–45	☐
20	Lev. 26–27	Mark 2	☐
21	Num. 1–2	Mark 3:1–19	☐
22	Num. 3–4	Mark 3:20–35	☐
23	Num. 5–6	Mark 4:1–20	☐
24	Num. 7–8	Mark 4:21–41	☐
25	Num. 9–11	Mark 5:1–20	☐
26	Num. 12–14	Mark 5:21–43	☐
27	Num. 15–16	Mark 6:1–29	☐
28	Num. 17–19	Mark 6:30–56	☐

March

Day	Old Testament	New Testament	✔
1	Num. 20–22	Mark 7:1–13	☐
2	Num. 23–25	Mark 7:14–37	☐
3	Num. 26–28	Mark 8	☐
4	Num. 29–31	Mark 9:1–29	☐
5	Num. 32–34	Mark 9:30–50	☐
6	Num. 35–36	Mark 10:1–31	☐
7	Deut. 1–3	Mark 10:32–52	☐
8	Deut. 4–6	Mark 11:1–18	☐
9	Deut. 7–9	Mark 11:19–33	☐
10	Deut. 10–12	Mark 12:1–27	☐
11	Deut. 13–15	Mark 12:28–44	☐
12	Deut. 16–18	Mark 13:1–20	☐
13	Deut. 19–21	Mark 13:21–37	☐
14	Deut. 22–24	Mark 14:1–26	☐
15	Deut. 25–27	Mark 14:27–53	☐
16	Deut. 28–29	Mark 14:54–72	☐
17	Deut. 30–31	Mark 15:1–25	☐
18	Deut. 32–34	Mark 15:26–47	☐
19	Josh. 1–3	Mark 16	☐
20	Josh. 4–6	Luke 1:1–20	☐
21	Josh. 7–9	Luke 1:21–38	☐
22	Josh. 10–12	Luke 1:39–56	☐
23	Josh. 13–15	Luke 1:57–80	☐
24	Josh. 16–18	Luke 2:1–24	☐
25	Josh. 19–21	Luke 2:25–52	☐
26	Josh. 22–24	Luke 3	☐
27	Judges 1–3	Luke 4:1–30	☐
28	Judges 4–6	Luke 4:31–44	☐
29	Judges 7–8	Luke 5:1–16	☐
30	Judges 9–10	Luke 5:17–39	☐
31	Judges 11–12	Luke 6:1–26	☐

April

Day	Old Testament	New Testament	✔
1	Judges 13–15	Luke 6:27–49	☐
2	Judges 16–18	Luke 7:1–30	☐
3	Judges 19–21	Luke 7:31–50	☐
4	Ruth 1–4	Luke 8:1–25	☐
5	1 Sam. 1–3	Luke 8:26–56	☐
6	1 Sam. 4–6	Luke 9:1–17	☐
7	1 Sam. 7–9	Luke 9:18–36	☐
8	1 Sam. 10–12	Luke 9:37–62	☐
9	1 Sam. 13–14	Luke 10:1–24	☐
10	1 Sam. 15–16	Luke 10:25–42	☐
11	1 Sam. 17–18	Luke 11:1–28	☐
12	1 Sam. 19–21	Luke 11:29–54	☐
13	1 Sam. 22–24	Luke 12:1–31	☐
14	1 Sam. 25–26	Luke 12:32–59	☐
15	1 Sam. 27–29	Luke 13:1–22	☐
16	1 Sam. 30–31	Luke 13:23–35	☐
17	2 Sam. 1–2	Luke 14:1–24	☐
18	2 Sam. 3–5	Luke 14:25–35	☐
19	2 Sam. 6–8	Luke 15:1–10	☐
20	2 Sam. 9–11	Luke 15:11–32	☐
21	2 Sam. 12–13	Luke 16	☐
22	2 Sam. 14–15	Luke 17:1–19	☐
23	2 Sam. 16–18	Luke 17:20–37	☐
24	2 Sam. 19–20	Luke 18:1–23	☐
25	2 Sam. 21–22	Luke 18:24–43	☐
26	2 Sam. 23–24	Luke 19:1–27	☐
27	1 Kings 1–2	Luke 19:28–48	☐
28	1 Kings 3–5	Luke 20:1–26	☐
29	1 Kings 6–7	Luke 20:27–47	☐
30	1 Kings 8–9	Luke 21:1–19	☐

May

Day	Old Testament	New Testament	✔
1	1 Kings 10–11	Luke 21:20–38	☐
2	1 Kings 12–13	Luke 22:1–30	☐
3	1 Kings 14–15	Luke 22:31–46	☐
4	1 Kings 16–18	Luke 22:47–71	☐
5	1 Kings 19–20	Luke 23:1–25	☐
6	1 Kings 21–22	Luke 23:26–56	☐
7	2 Kings 1–3	Luke 24:1–35	☐
8	2 Kings 4–6	Luke 24:36–53	☐
9	2 Kings 7–9	John 1:1–28	☐
10	2 Kings 10–12	John 1:29–51	☐
11	2 Kings 13–14	John 2	☐
12	2 Kings 15–16	John 3:1–18	☐
13	2 Kings 17–18	John 3:19–36	☐
14	2 Kings 19–21	John 4:1–30	☐
15	2 Kings 22–23	John 4:31–54	☐
16	2 Kings 24–25	John 5:1–24	☐
17	1 Chr. 1–3	John 5:25–47	☐
18	1 Chr. 4–6	John 6:1–21	☐
19	1 Chr. 7–9	John 6:22–44	☐
20	1 Chr. 10–12	John 6:45–71	☐
21	1 Chr. 13–15	John 7:1–27	☐
22	1 Chr. 16–18	John 7:28–53	☐
23	1 Chr. 19–21	John 8:1–27	☐
24	1 Chr. 22–24	John 8:28–59	☐
25	1 Chr. 25–27	John 9:1–23	☐
26	1 Chr. 28–29	John 9:24–41	☐
27	2 Chr. 1–3	John 10:1–23	☐
28	2 Chr. 4–6	John 10:24–42	☐
29	2 Chr. 7–9	John 11:1–29	☐
30	2 Chr. 10–12	John 11:30–57	☐
31	2 Chr. 13–14	John 12:1–26	☐

June

Day	Old Testament	New Testament	✔
1	2 Chr. 15–16	John 12:27–50	☐
2	2 Chr. 17–18	John 13:1–20	☐
3	2 Chr. 19–20	John 13:21–38	☐
4	2 Chr. 21–22	John 14	☐
5	2 Chr. 23–24	John 15	☐
6	2 Chr. 25–27	John 16	☐
7	2 Chr. 28–29	John 17	☐
8	2 Chr. 30–31	John 18:1–18	☐
9	2 Chr. 32–33	John 18:19–40	☐
10	2 Chr. 34–36	John 19:1–22	☐
11	Ezra 1–2	John 19:23–42	☐
12	Ezra 3–5	John 20	☐
13	Ezra 6–8	John 21	☐
14	Ezra 9–10	Acts 1	☐
15	Neh. 1–3	Acts 2:1–21	☐
16	Neh. 4–6	Acts 2:22–47	☐
17	Neh. 7–9	Acts 3	☐
18	Neh. 10–11	Acts 4:1–22	☐
19	Neh. 12–13	Acts 4:23–37	☐
20	Esther 1–2	Acts 5:1–21	☐
21	Esther 3–5	Acts 5:22–42	☐
22	Esther 6–8	Acts 6	☐
23	Esther 9–10	Acts 7:1–21	☐
24	Job 1–2	Acts 7:22–43	☐
25	Job 3–4	Acts 7:44–60	☐
26	Job 5–7	Acts 8:1–25	☐
27	Job 8–10	Acts 8:26–40	☐
28	Job 11–13	Acts 9:1–21	☐
29	Job 14–16	Acts 9:22–43	☐
30	Job 17–19	Acts 10:1–23	☐

July

Day	Old Testament	New Testament	✔
1	Job 20–21	Acts 10:24–48	❏
2	Job 22–24	Acts 11	❏
3	Job 25–27	Acts 12	❏
4	Job 28–29	Acts 13:1–25	❏
5	Job 30–31	Acts 13:26–52	❏
6	Job 32–33	Acts 14	❏
7	Job 34–35	Acts 15:1–21	❏
8	Job 36–37	Acts 15:22–41	❏
9	Job 38–40	Acts 16:1–21	❏
10	Job 41–42	Acts 16:22–40	❏
11	Ps. 1–3	Acts 17:1–15	❏
12	Ps. 4–6	Acts 17:16–34	❏
13	Ps. 7–9	Acts 18	❏
14	Ps. 10–12	Acts 19:1–20	❏
15	Ps. 13–15	Acts 19:21–41	❏
16	Ps. 16–17	Acts 20:1–16	❏
17	Ps. 18–19	Acts 20:17–38	❏
18	Ps. 20–22	Acts 21:1–17	❏
19	Ps. 23–25	Acts 21:18–40	❏
20	Ps. 26–28	Acts 22	❏
21	Ps. 29–30	Acts 23:1–15	❏
22	Ps. 31–32	Acts 23:16–35	❏
23	Ps. 33–34	Acts 24	❏
24	Ps. 35–36	Acts 25	❏
25	Ps. 37–39	Acts 26	❏
26	Ps. 40–42	Acts 27:1–26	❏
27	Ps. 43–45	Acts 27:27–44	❏
28	Ps. 46–48	Acts 28	❏
29	Ps. 49–50	Rom. 1	❏
30	Ps. 51–53	Rom. 2	❏
31	Ps. 54–56	Rom. 3	❏

August

Day	Old Testament	New Testament	✔
1	Ps. 57–59	Rom. 4	❏
2	Ps. 60–62	Rom. 5	❏
3	Ps. 63–65	Rom. 6	❏
4	Ps. 66–67	Rom. 7	❏
5	Ps. 68–69	Rom. 8:1–21	❏
6	Ps. 70–71	Rom. 8:22–39	❏
7	Ps. 72–73	Rom. 9:1–15	❏
8	Ps. 74–76	Rom. 9:16–33	❏
9	Ps. 77–78	Rom. 10	❏
10	Ps. 79–80	Rom. 11:1–18	❏
11	Ps. 81–83	Rom. 11:19–36	❏
12	Ps. 84–86	Rom. 12	❏
13	Ps. 87–88	Rom. 13	❏
14	Ps. 89–90	Rom. 14	❏
15	Ps. 91–93	Rom. 15:1–13	❏
16	Ps. 94–96	Rom. 15:14–33	❏
17	Ps. 97–99	Rom. 16	❏
18	Ps. 100–102	1 Cor. 1	❏
19	Ps. 103–104	1 Cor. 2	❏
20	Ps. 105–106	1 Cor. 3	❏
21	Ps. 107–109	1 Cor. 4	❏
22	Ps. 110–112	1 Cor. 5	❏
23	Ps. 113–115	1 Cor. 6	❏
24	Ps. 116–118	1 Cor. 7:1–19	❏
25	Ps. 119:1–88	1 Cor. 7:20–40	❏
26	Ps. 119:89–176	1 Cor. 8	❏
27	Ps. 120–122	1 Cor. 9	❏
28	Ps.123–125	1 Cor. 10:1–18	❏
29	Ps. 126–128	1 Cor. 10:19–33	❏
30	Ps. 129–131	1 Cor. 11:1–16	❏
31	Ps. 132–134	1 Cor. 11:17–34	❏

September

Day	Old Testament	New Testament	✔
1	Ps. 135–136	1 Cor. 12	❏
2	Ps. 137–139	1 Cor. 13	❏
3	Ps. 140–142	1 Cor. 14:1–20	❏
4	Ps. 143–145	1 Cor. 14:21–40	❏
5	Ps. 146–147	1 Cor. 15:1–28	❏
6	Ps. 148–150	1 Cor. 15:29–58	❏
7	Prov. 1–2	1 Cor. 16	❏
8	Prov. 3–5	2 Cor. 1	❏
9	Prov. 6–7	2 Cor. 2	❏
10	Prov. 8–9	2 Cor. 3	❏
11	Prov. 10–12	2 Cor. 4	❏
12	Prov. 13–15	2 Cor. 5	❏
13	Prov. 16–18	2 Cor. 6	❏
14	Prov. 19–21	2 Cor. 7	❏
15	Prov. 22–24	2 Cor. 8	❏
16	Prov. 25–26	2 Cor. 9	❏
17	Prov. 27–29	2 Cor. 10	❏
18	Prov. 30–31	2 Cor. 11:1–15	❏
19	Eccl. 1–3	2 Cor. 11:16–33	❏
20	Eccl. 4–6	2 Cor. 12	❏
21	Eccl. 7–9	2 Cor. 13	❏
22	Eccl. 10–12	Gal. 1	❏
23	Song 1–3	Gal. 2	❏
24	Song 4–5	Gal. 3	❏
25	Song 6–8	Gal. 4	❏
26	Isa. 1–2	Gal. 5	❏
27	Isa. 3–4	Gal. 6	❏
28	Isa. 5–6	Eph. 1	❏
29	Isa. 7–8	Eph. 2	❏
30	Isa. 9–10	Eph. 3	❏

October

Day	Old Testament	New Testament	✔
1	Isa. 11–13	Eph. 4	❏
2	Isa. 14–16	Eph. 5:1–16	❏
3	Isa. 17–19	Eph. 5:17–33	❏
4	Isa. 20–22	Eph. 6	❏
5	Isa. 23–25	Phil. 1	❏
6	Isa. 26–27	Phil. 2	❏
7	Isa. 28–29	Phil. 3	❏
8	Isa. 30–31	Phil. 4	❏
9	Isa. 32–33	Col. 1	❏
10	Isa. 34–36	Col. 2	❏
11	Isa. 37–38	Col. 3	❏
12	Isa. 39–40	Col. 4	❏
13	Isa. 41–42	1 Thess. 1	❏
14	Isa. 43–44	1 Thess. 2	❏
15	Isa. 45–46	1 Thess. 3	❏
16	Isa. 47–49	1 Thess. 4	❏
17	Isa. 50–52	1 Thess. 5	❏
18	Isa. 53–55	2 Thess. 1	❏
19	Isa. 56–58	2 Thess. 2	❏
20	Isa. 59–61	2 Thess. 3	❏
21	Isa. 62–64	1 Tim. 1	❏
22	Isa. 65–66	1 Tim. 2	❏
23	Jer. 1–2	1 Tim. 3	❏
24	Jer. 3–5	1 Tim. 4	❏
25	Jer. 6–8	1 Tim. 5	❏
26	Jer. 9–11	1 Tim. 6	❏
27	Jer. 12–14	2 Tim. 1	❏
28	Jer. 15–17	2 Tim. 2	❏
29	Jer. 18–19	2 Tim. 3	❏
30	Jer. 20–21	2 Tim. 4	❏
31	Jer. 22–23	Titus 1	❏

November

Day	Old Testament	New Testament	✔
1	Jer. 24–26	Titus 2	❏
2	Jer. 27–29	Titus 3	❏
3	Jer. 30–31	Philemon	❏
4	Jer. 32–33	Heb. 1	❏
5	Jer. 34–36	Heb. 2	❏
6	Jer. 37–39	Heb. 3	❏
7	Jer. 40–42	Heb. 4	❏
8	Jer. 43–45	Heb. 5	❏
9	Jer. 46–47	Heb. 6	❏
10	Jer. 48–49	Heb. 7	❏
11	Jer. 50	Heb. 8	❏
12	Jer. 51–52	Heb. 9	❏
13	Lam. 1–2	Heb. 10:1–18	❏
14	Lam. 3–5	Heb. 10:19–39	❏
15	Ezek. 1–2	Heb. 11:1–19	❏
16	Ezek. 3–4	Heb. 11:20–40	❏
17	Ezek. 5–7	Heb. 12	❏
18	Ezek. 8–10	Heb. 13	❏
19	Ezek. 11–13	James 1	❏
20	Ezek. 14–15	James 2	❏
21	Ezek. 16–17	James 3	❏
22	Ezek. 18–19	James 4	❏
23	Ezek. 20–21	James 5	❏
24	Ezek. 22–23	1 Peter 1	❏
25	Ezek. 24–26	1 Peter 2	❏
26	Ezek. 27–29	1 Peter 3	❏
27	Ezek. 30–32	1 Peter 4	❏
28	Ezek. 33–34	1 Peter 5	❏
29	Ezek. 35–36	2 Peter 1	❏
30	Ezek. 37–39	2 Peter 2	❏

December

Day	Old Testament	New Testament	✔
1	Ezek. 40–41	2 Peter 3	❏
2	Ezek. 42–44	1 John 1	❏
3	Ezek. 45–46	1 John 2	❏
4	Ezek. 47–48	1 John 3	❏
5	Dan. 1–2	1 John 4	❏
6	Dan. 3–4	1 John 5	❏
7	Dan. 5–7	2 John	❏
8	Dan. 8–10	3 John	❏
9	Dan. 11–12	Jude	❏
10	Hos. 1–4	Rev. 1	❏
11	Hos. 5–8	Rev. 2	❏
12	Hos. 9–11	Rev. 3	❏
13	Hos. 12–14	Rev. 4	❏
14	Joel	Rev. 5	❏
15	Amos 1–3	Rev. 6	❏
16	Amos 4–6	Rev. 7	❏
17	Amos 7–9	Rev. 8	❏
18	Obad.	Rev. 9	❏
19	Jonah	Rev. 10	❏
20	Micah 1–3	Rev. 11	❏
21	Micah 4–5	Rev. 12	❏
22	Micah 6–7	Rev. 13	❏
23	Nahum	Rev. 14	❏
24	Hab.	Rev. 15	❏
25	Zeph.	Rev. 16	❏
26	Hag.	Rev. 17	❏
27	Zech. 1–4	Rev. 18	❏
28	Zech. 5–8	Rev. 19	❏
29	Zech. 9–12	Rev. 20	❏
30	Zech. 13–14	Rev. 21	❏
31	Mal.	Rev. 22	❏

90-Day schedule

Day	Start	End	✔
1	Genesis 1:1	Genesis 16:16	❑
2	Genesis 17:1	Genesis 28:19	❑
3	Genesis 28:20	Genesis 40:11	❑
4	Genesis 40:12	Genesis 50:26	❑
5	Exodus 1:1	Exodus 15:18	❑
6	Exodus 15:19	Exodus 28:43	❑
7	Exodus 29:1	Exodus 40:38	❑
8	Leviticus 1:1	Leviticus 14:32	❑
9	Leviticus 14:33	Leviticus 26:26	❑
10	Leviticus 26:27	Numbers 8:14	❑
11	Numbers 8:15	Numbers 21:7	❑
12	Numbers 21:8	Numbers 32:19	❑
13	Numbers 32:20	Deuteronomy 7:26	❑
14	Deuteronomy 8:1	Deuteronomy 23:11	❑
15	Deuteronomy 23:12	Deuteronomy 34:12	❑
16	Joshua 1:1	Joshua 14:15	❑
17	Joshua 15:1	Judges 3:27	❑
18	Judges 3:28	Judges 15:12	❑
19	Judges 15:13	1 Samuel 2:29	❑
20	1 Samuel 2:30	1 Samuel 15:35	❑
21	1 Samuel 16:1	1 Samuel 28:19	❑
22	1 Samuel 28:20	2 Samuel 12:10	❑
23	2 Samuel 12:11	2 Samuel 22:18	❑
24	2 Samuel 22:19	1 Kings 7:37	❑
25	1 Kings 7:38	1 Kings 16:20	❑
26	1 Kings 16:21	2 Kings 4:37	❑
27	2 Kings 4:38	2 Kings 15:26	❑
28	2 Kings 15:27	2 Kings 25:30	❑
29	1 Chronicles 1:1	1 Chronicles 9:44	❑
30	1 Chronicles 10:1	1 Chronicles 23:32	❑
31	1 Chronicles 24:1	2 Chronicles 7:10	❑
32	2 Chronicles 7:11	2 Chronicles 23:15	❑
33	2 Chronicles 23:16	2 Chronicles 35:15	❑
34	2 Chronicles 35:16	Ezra 10:44	❑
35	Nehemiah 1:1	Nehemiah 13:14	❑
36	Nehemiah 13:15	Job 7:21	❑
37	Job 8:1	Job 24:25	❑
38	Job 25:1	Job 41:34	❑
39	Job 42:1	Psalm 24:10	❑
40	Psalm 25:1	Psalm 45:14	❑
41	Psalm 45:15	Psalm 69:21	❑
42	Psalm 69:22	Psalm 89:13	❑
43	Psalm 89:14	Psalm 108:13	❑
44	Psalm 109:1	Psalm 134:3	❑
45	Psalm 135:1	Proverbs 6:35	❑
46	Proverbs 7:1	Proverbs 20:21	❑
47	Proverbs 20:22	Ecclesiastes 2:26	❑
48	Ecclesiastes 3:1	Song 8:14	❑
49	Isaiah 1:1	Isaiah 13:22	❑
50	Isaiah 14:1	Isaiah 28:29	❑
51	Isaiah 29:1	Isaiah 41:18	❑
52	Isaiah 41:19	Isaiah 52:12	❑
53	Isaiah 52:13	Isaiah 66:18	❑
54	Isaiah 66:19	Jeremiah 10:13	❑
55	Jeremiah 10:14	Jeremiah 23:8	❑
56	Jeremiah 23:9	Jeremiah 33:22	❑
57	Jeremiah 33:23	Jeremiah 47:7	❑
58	Jeremiah 48:1	Lamentations 1:22	❑
59	Lamentations 2:1	Ezekiel 12:20	❑
60	Ezekiel 12:21	Ezekiel 23:39	❑
61	Ezekiel 23:40	Ezekiel 35:15	❑
62	Ezekiel 36:1	Ezekiel 47:12	❑
63	Ezekiel 47:13	Daniel 8:27	❑
64	Daniel 9:1	Hosea 13:6	❑
65	Hosea 13:7	Amos 9:10	❑
66	Amos 9:11	Nahum 3:19	❑
67	Habakkuk 1:1	Zechariah 10:12	❑
68	Zechariah 11:1	Matthew 4:25	❑
69	Matthew 5:1	Matthew 15:39	❑
70	Matthew 16:1	Matthew 26:56	❑
71	Matthew 26:57	Mark 9:13	❑
72	Mark 9:14	Luke 1:80	❑
73	Luke 2:1	Luke 9:62	❑
74	Luke 10:1	Luke 20:19	❑
75	Luke 20:20	John 5:47	❑
76	John 6:1	John 15:17	❑
77	John 15:18	Acts 6:7	❑
78	Acts 6:8	Acts 16:37	❑
79	Acts 16:38	Acts 28:16	❑
80	Acts 28:17	Romans 14:23	❑
81	Romans 15:1	1 Corinthians 14:40	❑
82	1 Corinthians 15:1	Galatians 3:25	❑
83	Galatians 3:26	Colossians 4:18	❑
84	1 Thessalonians 1:1	Philemon 25	❑
85	Hebrews 1:1	James 3:12	❑
86	James 3:13	3 John 14	❑
87	Jude 1	Revelation 17:18	❑
88	Revelation 18:1	Revelation 22:21	❑
89	Grace Day	Grace Day	❑
90	Grace Day	Grace Day	❑

SEVEN
Prayer List

Perhaps my favorite Bible verse in all of Scripture is Jeremiah 33:3, *"Call unto me, and I will answer thee, and show thee great and mighty things, which thou knowest not."* It is my prayer that this section of your journal will especially encourage you in your walk with God as you call on Him and record the great and mighty things He accomplishes for and through you.

I've divided this prayer list section into three parts: a daily prayer list, a weekly prayer list, and a specific prayer list.

Daily Prayer List

There are many things I pray for on a daily basis. I pray for myself, for instance, that I would be sensitive to the Holy Spirit and obedient to do His will. I pray through my roles as a child of God, wife, mom, teacher, and friend. I also pray for my husband, children, and grandchildren. In this portion of your prayer list, I encourage you to record similar daily prayer requests to the Lord. You can also use this section as a personal checklist in prayer as you seek to keep your heart right with the Lord each day.

Weekly Prayer List

I know many people who enjoy dividing their prayer list by days of the week. Perhaps you pray for missionaries in certain regions of the world on a specific day. Or, you may want to spend extra time in prayer one day per week for specific family members. You may focus your heart in prayer on Saturdays for various ministries that take place in your church on Sundays. You get the idea. We've left these pages blank, so you can customize or create headings according to your preference.

Specific Prayer List

This third section of my daily prayer list is perhaps the most fun to record. In these pages, write specific prayer requests that require help and answers from the Lord. As you record the date you began praying and the date God answered your prayer, your faith will be strengthened and your confidence in God's faithfulness will increase. Imagine the joy that will fill your heart as you look back over your prayer list at the end of the year and remember how He specifically worked in your life in special ways.

daily prayer list

daily prayer list

daily prayer list

weekly prayer list

weekly prayer list

weekly prayer list

weekly prayer list

weekly prayer list

weekly prayer list

weekly prayer list

weekly prayer list

specific prayer list

date	request	date answered

date	request	date answered

date	request	date answered

date	request	date answered

date	request	date answered

date	request	date answered

date	request	date answered

date	request	date answered

date	*request*	*date answered*

EIGHT
Notes

_____

_____

_____

_____

_____

_____

_____

_____

_____

_____

_____

_____

_____

PART TWO

Give Your Day a Wonderful Start

TODAY'S A
WONDERFUL DAY

TODAY'S DATE 11 / 4 / 17

notes

passage I read:

truths for my day:
Luke loves me.

today I'm thankful for:
my mom - her birthday!
a trip
biblical messages
healthy baby girl
coffee ☺

This is the day which the LORD hath made; we will rejoice and be glad in it.—Psalm 118:24

TODAY'S A
WONDERFUL DAY

TODAY'S DATE 1 , 26 , 18

passage I read:

psalm 40

i love verses 1-5.
they have always
been special to me.

truths for my day:

i am alive
i am healthy
i live in USA!
i have a great family
i have a beautiful home

today I'm thankful for: ➤

God's mercies

notes

Found some
amazing
pottery i've been
wanting for cheap!

got some new shoes
& clothes for dirt
cheap!

had fun with
Luke + Brooke
at Dunkin

got a massage!

had an overall
good day!

But his delight is in the law of the LORD; and in his law doth he meditate day and night.—Psalm 1:2

meditate on the scriptures ♥

TODAY'S A
WONDERFUL DAY

TODAY'S DATE _____ /_____ /_____

notes

passage I read:

_____

_____

_____

_____

_____

_____

_____

truths for my day:

_____

_____

_____

_____

_____

_____

_____

today I'm thankful for:

_____

_____

_____

_____

_____

I will praise thee; for I am fearfully and wonderfully made: marvellous are thy works; and that my soul knoweth right well.—Psalm 139:14

TODAY'S A
WONDERFUL DAY

TODAY'S DATE _____ / _____ / _____

passage I read:

_____

_____

_____

_____

_____

_____

_____

truths for my day:

_____

_____

_____

_____

_____

_____

_____

today I'm thankful for:

_____

_____

_____

_____

_____

notes

Good and upright is the Lord: therefore will he teach sinners in the way.—Psalm 25:8

TODAY'S A
WONDERFUL DAY

TODAY'S DATE _____ / _____ / _____

notes

passage I read:

_____
_____
_____
_____
_____
_____
_____
_____

truths for my day:

_____
_____
_____
_____
_____
_____
_____
_____

today I'm thankful for:

_____
_____
_____
_____
_____

Thou wilt keep him in perfect peace, whose mind is stayed on thee:
because he trusteth in thee.—Isaiah 26:3

TODAY'S A
WONDERFUL DAY

TODAY'S DATE _____ / _____ / _____

passage I read:

_____
_____
_____
_____
_____
_____
_____

truths for my day:

_____
_____
_____
_____
_____
_____
_____

today I'm thankful for:

_____
_____
_____
_____
_____

notes

I had fainted, unless I had believed to see the goodness of the LORD in the land of the living.—Psalm 27:13

TODAY'S A
WONDERFUL DAY

TODAY'S DATE _____ / _____ / _____

notes

passage I read:

_____
_____
_____
_____
_____
_____
_____

truths for my day:

_____
_____
_____
_____
_____
_____
_____

today I'm thankful for:

_____
_____
_____
_____

*The LORD hear thee in the day of trouble; the name of the God of
Jacob defend thee;—Psalm 20:1*

TODAY'S A
WONDERFUL DAY

TODAY'S DATE _____ / _____ / _____

passage I read:

_____
_____
_____
_____
_____
_____
_____

truths for my day:

_____
_____
_____
_____
_____
_____
_____

today I'm thankful for:

_____
_____
_____
_____

notes

Oh that men would praise the LORD for his goodness, and for his wonderful works to the children of men!—Psalm 107:8

TODAY'S A
WONDERFUL DAY

TODAY'S DATE _____ / _____ / _____

notes

passage I read:

_____
_____
_____
_____
_____
_____
_____

truths for my day:

_____
_____
_____
_____
_____
_____

today I'm thankful for:

_____
_____
_____
_____

Trust in the LORD with all thine heart; and lean not unto thine own understanding. In all thy ways acknowledge him, and he shall direct thy paths.—Proverbs 3:5–6

TODAY'S A
WONDERFUL DAY

TODAY'S DATE _____ / _____ / _____

passage I read:

_____

_____

_____

_____

_____

_____

truths for my day:

_____

_____

_____

_____

_____

_____

_____

today I'm thankful for:

_____

_____

_____

_____

notes

Peace I leave with you, my peace I give unto you: not as the world giveth, give I unto you.
Let not your heart be troubled, neither let it be afraid.—John 14:27

TODAY'S A
WONDERFUL DAY

TODAY'S DATE _____ / _____ / _____

notes

passage I read:

_____
_____
_____
_____
_____
_____
_____

truths for my day:

_____
_____
_____
_____
_____
_____

today I'm thankful for:

_____
_____
_____
_____

For I know the thoughts that I think toward you, saith the LORD, thoughts of peace,
and not of evil, to give you an expected end.—Jeremiah 29:11

TODAY'S A
WONDERFUL DAY

TODAY'S DATE _____ / _____ / _____

passage I read:

_____

_____

_____

_____

_____

_____

_____

truths for my day:

_____

_____

_____

_____

_____

_____

today I'm thankful for:

_____

_____

_____

_____

notes

Many, O Lord my God, are thy wonderful works which thou hast done, and thy
thoughts which are to us-ward: they cannot be reckoned up in order unto thee: if I would
declare and speak of them, they are more than can be numbered.—Psalm 40:5

TODAY'S A
WONDERFUL DAY

TODAY'S DATE _____ /_____ /_____

notes

passage I read:

_____
_____
_____
_____
_____
_____
_____
_____

truths for my day:

_____
_____
_____
_____
_____
_____
_____
_____

today I'm thankful for:

_____
_____
_____
_____
_____
_____

Praise the LORD; for the LORD is good: sing praises unto his name;
for it is pleasant.—Psalm 135:3

TODAY'S A
WONDERFUL DAY

TODAY'S DATE _____ /_____ /_____

passage I read:

_____
_____
_____
_____
_____
_____
_____

truths for my day:

_____
_____
_____
_____
_____
_____
_____

today I'm thankful for:

_____
_____
_____
_____
_____

notes

For he satisfieth the longing soul, and filleth the hungry soul with goodness.—Psalm 107:9

TODAY'S A
WONDERFUL DAY

TODAY'S DATE _____ / _____ / _____

notes

passage I read:

_____
_____
_____
_____
_____
_____
_____

truths for my day:

_____
_____
_____
_____
_____
_____
_____

today I'm thankful for:

_____
_____
_____
_____
_____

The Lord is good to all: and his tender mercies are over all his works.—Psalm 145:9

TODAY'S A
WONDERFUL DAY

TODAY'S DATE _____ / _____ / _____

passage I read:

_____
_____
_____
_____
_____
_____
_____
_____

truths for my day:

_____
_____
_____
_____
_____
_____
_____
_____

today I'm thankful for:

_____
_____
_____
_____

notes

Teach me to do thy will; for thou art my God: thy spirit is good; lead me into the land of uprightness.—Psalm 143:10

TODAY'S A
WONDERFUL DAY

TODAY'S DATE _____ / _____ / _____

notes

passage I read:

truths for my day:

today I'm thankful for:

For the LORD God is a sun and shield: the LORD will give grace and glory: no good thing will
he withhold from them that walk uprightly. —Psalm 84:11

TODAY'S A
WONDERFUL DAY

TODAY'S DATE _____ / _____ / _____

passage I read:

_____
_____
_____
_____
_____
_____
_____
_____

truths for my day:

_____
_____
_____
_____
_____
_____
_____
_____

today I'm thankful for:

_____
_____
_____
_____
_____

notes

Praise ye the LORD. O give thanks unto the LORD; for he is good:
for his mercy endureth for ever.—Psalm 106:1

TODAY'S A WONDERFUL DAY

TODAY'S DATE _____ /_____ /_____

notes

passage I read:

truths for my day:

today I'm thankful for:

For the LORD is good; his mercy is everlasting; and his truth
endureth to all generations.—Psalm 100:5

TODAY'S A
WONDERFUL DAY

TODAY'S DATE _____ / _____ / _____

passage I read:

_____

_____

_____

_____

_____

_____

_____

_____

truths for my day:

_____

_____

_____

_____

_____

_____

_____

_____

today I'm thankful for:

_____

_____

_____

_____

_____

notes

But it is good for me to draw near to God: I have put my trust in the LORD God,
that I may declare all thy works.—Psalm 73:28

TODAY'S A
WONDERFUL DAY

TODAY'S DATE _____ /_____ /_____

notes

passage I read:

_____
_____
_____
_____
_____
_____
_____
_____

truths for my day:

_____
_____
_____
_____
_____
_____
_____
_____

today I'm thankful for:

_____
_____
_____
_____
_____

Oh how great is thy goodness, which thou hast laid up for them that fear thee; which thou hast wrought for them that trust in thee before the sons of men!—Psalm 31:19

TODAY'S A
WONDERFUL DAY

TODAY'S DATE _____ /_____ /_____

passage I read:

_____
_____
_____
_____
_____
_____
_____
_____

truths for my day:

_____
_____
_____
_____
_____
_____
_____
_____

today I'm thankful for:

_____
_____
_____
_____
_____

notes

Blessed be the LORD God, the God of Israel, who only doeth wondrous things.—Psalm 72:18

TODAY'S A
WONDERFUL DAY

TODAY'S DATE _____ / _____ / _____

notes

passage I read:

_____
_____
_____
_____
_____
_____
_____

truths for my day:

_____
_____
_____
_____
_____
_____

today I'm thankful for:

_____
_____
_____
_____

He restoreth my soul: he leadeth me in the paths of righteousness for his name's sake.—
Psalm 23:3

TODAY'S A
WONDERFUL DAY

TODAY'S DATE _____ / _____ / _____

passage I read:

notes

_____

_____

_____

_____

_____

_____

_____

_____

truths for my day:

_____

_____

_____

_____

_____

_____

_____

today I'm thankful for:

_____

_____

_____

_____

_____

Be of good courage, and he shall strengthen your heart,
all ye that hope in the LORD.—Psalm 31:24

TODAY'S A
WONDERFUL DAY

TODAY'S DATE _____ / _____ / _____

notes

passage I read:

_____
_____
_____
_____
_____
_____
_____
_____
_____

truths for my day:

_____
_____
_____
_____
_____
_____
_____
_____
_____

today I'm thankful for:

_____
_____
_____
_____
_____

Thy testimonies are wonderful: therefore doth my soul keep them.—Psalm 119:129

TODAY'S A WONDERFUL DAY

TODAY'S DATE _____ / _____ / _____

passage I read:

_____
_____
_____
_____
_____
_____
_____

truths for my day:

_____
_____
_____
_____
_____
_____

today I'm thankful for:

_____
_____
_____
_____
_____

notes

Fear thou not; for I am with thee: be not dismayed; for I am thy God: I will strengthen thee; yea,
I will help thee; yea, I will uphold thee with the right hand of my righteousness.—Isaiah 41:10

TODAY'S A WONDERFUL DAY

TODAY'S DATE _____ / _____ / _____

notes

passage I read:
_____
_____
_____
_____
_____
_____
_____

truths for my day:
_____
_____
_____
_____
_____
_____

today I'm thankful for:
_____
_____
_____
_____

He hath made his wonderful works to be remembered: the LORD is gracious and full of compassion.—Psalm 111:4

TODAY'S A
WONDERFUL DAY

TODAY'S DATE _____ / _____ / _____

passage I read:

_____
_____
_____
_____
_____
_____
_____
_____

truths for my day:

_____
_____
_____
_____
_____
_____
_____

today I'm thankful for:

_____
_____
_____
_____
_____

notes

Surely goodness and mercy shall follow me all the days of my life: and I will dwell in the house of the LORD for ever.—Psalm 23:6

TODAY'S A
WONDERFUL DAY

TODAY'S DATE _____ /_____ /_____

notes

passage I read:

_____
_____
_____
_____
_____
_____
_____

truths for my day:

_____
_____
_____
_____
_____
_____

today I'm thankful for:

_____
_____
_____
_____

Trust in the LORD, and do good; so shalt thou dwell in the land,
and verily thou shalt be fed. —Psalm 37:3

TODAY'S A
WONDERFUL DAY

TODAY'S DATE _____ / _____ / _____

passage I read:

_____
_____
_____
_____
_____
_____
_____
_____

truths for my day:

_____
_____
_____
_____
_____
_____
_____

today I'm thankful for:

_____
_____
_____
_____
_____

notes

Hear me, O LORD; for thy lovingkindness is good: turn unto me according
to the multitude of thy tender mercies.—Psalm 69:16

TODAY'S A
WONDERFUL DAY

TODAY'S DATE _____ /_____ /_____

notes

passage I read:

_____
_____
_____
_____
_____
_____
_____

truths for my day:

_____
_____
_____
_____
_____
_____
_____

today I'm thankful for:

_____
_____
_____
_____
_____

Lead me in thy truth, and teach me: for thou art the God of my salvation;
on thee do I wait all the day.—Psalm 25:5

TODAY'S A
WONDERFUL DAY

TODAY'S DATE _____ / _____ / _____

passage I read:

_____
_____
_____
_____
_____
_____
_____
_____

truths for my day:

_____
_____
_____
_____
_____
_____
_____

today I'm thankful for:

_____
_____
_____
_____
_____

notes

O taste and see that the Lord is good: blessed is the man that trusteth in him.—Psalm 34:8

TODAY'S A
WONDERFUL DAY

TODAY'S DATE _____ / _____ / _____

notes

passage I read:

_____
_____
_____
_____
_____
_____
_____

truths for my day:

_____
_____
_____
_____
_____
_____
_____

today I'm thankful for:

_____
_____
_____
_____
_____

One thing have I desired of the LORD, that will I seek after; that I may dwell in the house of the LORD all the days of my life, to behold the beauty of the LORD, and to enquire in his temple.—Psalm 27:4

TODAY'S A
WONDERFUL DAY

TODAY'S DATE _____ / _____ / _____

passage I read:

notes

_____
_____
_____
_____
_____
_____
_____

truths for my day:

_____
_____
_____
_____
_____
_____

today I'm thankful for:

_____
_____
_____
_____
_____

All the paths of the LORD are mercy and truth unto such as keep
his covenant and his testimonies.—Psalm 25:10

TODAY'S A
WONDERFUL DAY

TODAY'S DATE _____ / _____ / _____

notes

passage I read:

_____
_____
_____
_____
_____
_____
_____
_____

truths for my day:

_____
_____
_____
_____
_____
_____
_____

today I'm thankful for:

_____
_____
_____
_____
_____

Unto thee, O God, do we give thanks, unto thee do we give thanks: for that thy name is near thy wondrous works declare.—Psalm 75:1

TODAY'S A
WONDERFUL DAY

TODAY'S DATE _____ / _____ / _____

passage I read:

_____
_____
_____
_____
_____
_____
_____
_____

truths for my day:

_____
_____
_____
_____
_____
_____
_____
_____

today I'm thankful for:

_____
_____
_____
_____
_____
_____

notes

And my tongue shall speak of thy righteousness and of thy praise all the day long.—Psalm 35:28

TODAY'S A
WONDERFUL DAY

TODAY'S DATE _____ / _____ / _____

notes

passage I read:

_____
_____
_____
_____
_____
_____
_____

truths for my day:

_____
_____
_____
_____
_____
_____
_____

today I'm thankful for:

_____
_____
_____
_____
_____

Yet the Lord will command his lovingkindness in the day time, and in the night his song shall be with me,
and my prayer unto the God of my life.—Psalm 42:8

TODAY'S A WONDERFUL DAY

TODAY'S DATE _____ / _____ / _____

passage I read:

_____
_____
_____
_____
_____
_____
_____
_____

truths for my day:

_____
_____
_____
_____
_____
_____
_____
_____

today I'm thankful for:

_____
_____
_____
_____
_____
_____

notes

And call upon me in the day of trouble: I will deliver thee, and thou shalt glorify me.—Psalm 50:15

TODAY'S A
WONDERFUL DAY

TODAY'S DATE _____ / _____ / _____

notes

passage I read:

_____
_____
_____
_____
_____
_____
_____

truths for my day:

_____
_____
_____
_____
_____
_____
_____

today I'm thankful for:

_____
_____
_____
_____
_____

God is our refuge and strength, a very present help in trouble. Therefore will not we fear, though the earth be removed, and though the mountains be carried into the midst of the sea; Though the waters thereof roar and be troubled, though the mountains shake with the swelling thereof. Selah.—Psalm 46:1–3

TODAY'S A
WONDERFUL DAY

TODAY'S DATE _____ / _____ / _____

passage I read:

_____

_____

_____

_____

_____

_____

_____

_____

truths for my day:

_____

_____

_____

_____

_____

_____

_____

today I'm thankful for:

_____

_____

_____

_____

notes

Make me to understand the way of thy precepts: so shall I talk of thy wondrous works.—Psalm 119:27

TODAY'S A
WONDERFUL DAY

TODAY'S DATE _____ / _____ / _____

notes

passage I read:

_____
_____
_____
_____
_____
_____
_____
_____

truths for my day:

_____
_____
_____
_____
_____
_____
_____
_____

today I'm thankful for:

_____
_____
_____
_____

For thou art great, and doest wondrous things: thou art God alone.—Psalm 86:10

TODAY'S A
WONDERFUL DAY

TODAY'S DATE _____ / _____ / _____

passage I read:

_____
_____
_____
_____
_____
_____
_____
_____

truths for my day:

_____
_____
_____
_____
_____
_____
_____

today I'm thankful for:

_____
_____
_____
_____

notes

But I will sing of thy power; yea, I will sing aloud of thy mercy in the morning: for thou hast been my defence and refuge in the day of my trouble.—Psalm 59:16

TODAY'S A
WONDERFUL DAY

TODAY'S DATE _____ / _____ / _____

notes

passage I read:

truths for my day:

today I'm thankful for:

Let my mouth be filled with thy praise and with thy honour all the day.—Psalm 71:8

TODAY'S A
WONDERFUL DAY

TODAY'S DATE _____ / _____ / _____

passage I read:

_____

_____

_____

_____

_____

_____

_____

_____

truths for my day:

_____

_____

_____

_____

_____

_____

_____

today I'm thankful for:

_____

_____

_____

_____

_____

notes

My tongue also shall talk of thy righteousness all the day long...—Psalm 71:24

TODAY'S A
WONDERFUL DAY

TODAY'S DATE _____ / _____ / _____

notes

passage I read:

_____
_____
_____
_____
_____
_____
_____

truths for my day:

_____
_____
_____
_____
_____
_____
_____

today I'm thankful for:

_____
_____
_____
_____

I will speak of the glorious honour of thy majesty, and of thy
wondrous works.—Psalm 145:5

TODAY'S A WONDERFUL DAY

TODAY'S DATE _____ / _____ / _____

passage I read:

_____
_____
_____
_____
_____
_____
_____

truths for my day:

_____
_____
_____
_____
_____
_____
_____

today I'm thankful for:

_____
_____
_____
_____
_____

notes

In the day of my trouble I will call upon thee: for thou wilt answer me.—Psalm 86:7

TODAY'S A
WONDERFUL DAY

TODAY'S DATE _____ / _____ / _____

notes

passage I read:

_____
_____
_____
_____
_____
_____
_____
_____

truths for my day:

_____
_____
_____
_____
_____
_____
_____
_____

today I'm thankful for:

_____
_____
_____
_____
_____

So teach us to number our days, that we may apply our hearts
unto wisdom.—Psalm 90:12

TODAY'S A
WONDERFUL DAY

TODAY'S DATE _____ / _____ / _____

passage I read:

_____
_____
_____
_____
_____
_____
_____
_____

truths for my day:

_____
_____
_____
_____
_____
_____
_____

today I'm thankful for:

_____
_____
_____
_____
_____

notes

Open thou mine eyes, that I may behold wondrous things out of thy law.—Psalm 119:18

TODAY'S A
WONDERFUL DAY

TODAY'S DATE _____ / _____ / _____

notes

passage I read:

_____
_____
_____
_____
_____
_____
_____

truths for my day:

_____
_____
_____
_____
_____
_____
_____

today I'm thankful for:

_____
_____
_____
_____

O satisfy us early with thy mercy; that we may rejoice and be glad all our days—Psalm 90:14

TODAY'S A
WONDERFUL DAY

TODAY'S DATE _____ / _____ / _____

passage I read:

_____
_____
_____
_____
_____
_____
_____

truths for my day:

_____
_____
_____
_____
_____
_____
_____

today I'm thankful for:

_____
_____
_____
_____
_____

notes

*Sing unto the LORD, bless his name; shew forth his salvation
from day to day.*—Psalm 96:2

TODAY'S A WONDERFUL DAY

TODAY'S DATE _____ / _____ / _____

notes

passage I read:

_____
_____
_____
_____
_____
_____
_____

truths for my day:

_____
_____
_____
_____
_____
_____
_____

today I'm thankful for:

_____
_____
_____
_____
_____

Sing unto him, sing psalms unto him: talk ye of all his wondrous works.—Psalm 105:2

TODAY'S A
WONDERFUL DAY

TODAY'S DATE _____ / _____ / _____

passage I read:

_____

_____

_____

_____

_____

_____

_____

truths for my day:

_____

_____

_____

_____

_____

_____

today I'm thankful for:

_____

_____

_____

_____

notes

This is the day which the L<small>ORD</small> hath made; we will rejoice and be glad in it.—Psalm 118:24

TODAY'S A WONDERFUL DAY

TODAY'S DATE _____ / _____ / _____

notes

passage I read:

_____
_____
_____
_____
_____
_____
_____
_____

truths for my day:

_____
_____
_____
_____
_____
_____
_____
_____

today I'm thankful for:

_____
_____
_____
_____
_____
_____

O how love I thy law! it is my meditation all the day.—Psalm 119:97

TODAY'S A
WONDERFUL DAY

TODAY'S DATE _____ / _____ / _____

passage I read:

_____

_____

_____

_____

_____

_____

_____

truths for my day:

_____

_____

_____

_____

_____

_____

today I'm thankful for:

_____

_____

_____

_____

_____

notes

O God, thou hast taught me from my youth: and hitherto have I declared thy
wondrous works.—Psalm 71:17

TODAY'S A
WONDERFUL DAY

TODAY'S DATE _____ / _____ / _____

notes

passage I read:

_____
_____
_____
_____
_____
_____
_____
_____

truths for my day:

_____
_____
_____
_____
_____
_____
_____

today I'm thankful for:

_____
_____
_____
_____
_____

*In the day when I cried thou answeredst me, and strengthenedst me
with strength in my soul.—Psalm 138:3*

TODAY'S A
WONDERFUL DAY

TODAY'S DATE _____ / _____ / _____

passage I read:

_____

_____

_____

_____

_____

_____

_____

truths for my day:

_____

_____

_____

_____

_____

_____

today I'm thankful for:

_____

_____

_____

_____

_____

notes

Every day will I bless thee; and I will praise thy name for ever and ever.—Psalm 145:2

TODAY'S A
WONDERFUL DAY

TODAY'S DATE _____ / _____ / _____

notes

passage I read:

....

....

....

....

....

....

....

truths for my day:

....

....

....

....

....

....

....

today I'm thankful for:

....

....

....

....

Casting all your care upon him; for he careth for you. —1 Peter 5:7

TODAY'S A
WONDERFUL DAY

TODAY'S DATE _____ /_____ /_____

passage I read:

_____

_____

_____

_____

_____

_____

_____

truths for my day:

_____

_____

_____

_____

_____

_____

today I'm thankful for:

_____

_____

_____

_____

notes

But his delight is in the law of the LORD; and in his law doth he meditate day and night.—Psalm 1:2

TODAY'S A
WONDERFUL DAY

TODAY'S DATE _____ / _____ / _____

notes

passage I read:

_____
_____
_____
_____
_____
_____
_____
_____

truths for my day:

_____
_____
_____
_____
_____
_____
_____
_____

today I'm thankful for:

_____
_____
_____
_____
_____

I will praise thee; for I am fearfully and wonderfully made: marvellous are thy works; and that my soul knoweth right well.—Psalm 139:14

TODAY'S A
WONDERFUL DAY

TODAY'S DATE _____ /_____ /_____

passage I read:

_____
_____
_____
_____
_____
_____
_____
_____

truths for my day:

_____
_____
_____
_____
_____
_____
_____
_____

today I'm thankful for:

_____
_____
_____
_____
_____

Good and upright is the Lord: *therefore will he teach sinners in the way.*—Psalm 25:8

TODAY'S A
WONDERFUL DAY

TODAY'S DATE _____ /_____ /_____

notes

passage I read:

truths for my day:

today I'm thankful for:

Thou wilt keep him in perfect peace, whose mind is stayed on thee:
because he trusteth in thee.—Isaiah 26:3

TODAY'S A
WONDERFUL DAY

TODAY'S DATE _____ / _____ / _____

passage I read:

_____

_____

_____

_____

_____

_____

_____

_____

_____

truths for my day:

_____

_____

_____

_____

_____

_____

_____

today I'm thankful for:

_____

_____

_____

_____

_____

notes

I had fainted, unless I had believed to see the goodness of the LORD in the land of the living.—Psalm 27:13

TODAY'S A
WONDERFUL DAY

TODAY'S DATE _____ / _____ / _____

notes

passage I read:

truths for my day:

today I'm thankful for:

The LORD hear thee in the day of trouble; the name of the God of Jacob defend thee;—Psalm 20:1

TODAY'S A
WONDERFUL DAY

TODAY'S DATE _____ / _____ / _____

passage I read:

_____

_____

_____

_____

_____

_____

_____

truths for my day:

_____

_____

_____

_____

_____

_____

today I'm thankful for:

_____

_____

_____

_____

notes

Oh that men would praise the Lord *for his goodness, and for his wonderful works to the children of men!*—Psalm 107:8

TODAY'S A
WONDERFUL DAY

TODAY'S DATE _____ / _____ / _____

notes

passage I read:

_____
_____
_____
_____
_____
_____
_____

truths for my day:

_____
_____
_____
_____
_____
_____
_____
_____

today I'm thankful for:

_____
_____
_____
_____
_____

Trust in the Lord with all thine heart; and lean not unto thine own understanding. In all thy ways acknowledge him, and he shall direct thy paths.—Proverbs 3:5–6

TODAY'S A
WONDERFUL DAY

TODAY'S DATE _____ / _____ / _____

passage I read:

_____
_____
_____
_____
_____
_____
_____

truths for my day:

_____
_____
_____
_____
_____
_____
_____

today I'm thankful for:

_____
_____
_____
_____

notes

Peace I leave with you, my peace I give unto you: not as the world giveth, give I unto you.
Let not your heart be troubled, neither let it be afraid.—John 14:27

TODAY'S A WONDERFUL DAY

TODAY'S DATE _____ / _____ / _____

notes

passage I read:

truths for my day:

today I'm thankful for:

For I know the thoughts that I think toward you, saith the LORD, thoughts of peace,
and not of evil, to give you an expected end.—Jeremiah 29:11

TODAY'S A
WONDERFUL DAY

TODAY'S DATE _____ / _____ / _____

passage I read:

_____
_____
_____
_____
_____
_____
_____

truths for my day:

_____
_____
_____
_____
_____
_____

today I'm thankful for:

_____
_____
_____
_____
_____

notes

Many, O LORD my God, are thy wonderful works which thou hast done, and thy thoughts which are to us-ward: they cannot be reckoned up in order unto thee: if I would declare and speak of them, they are more than can be numbered. —Psalm 40:5

TODAY'S A
WONDERFUL DAY

TODAY'S DATE _____ / _____ / _____

notes

passage I read:

_____
_____
_____
_____
_____
_____
_____

truths for my day:

_____
_____
_____
_____
_____
_____
_____

today I'm thankful for:

_____
_____
_____
_____
_____

Praise the LORD; for the LORD is good: sing praises unto his name;
for it is pleasant.—Psalm 135:3

TODAY'S A
WONDERFUL DAY

TODAY'S DATE _____ /_____ /_____

passage I read:

_____
_____
_____
_____
_____
_____
_____
_____

truths for my day:

_____
_____
_____
_____
_____
_____
_____
_____

today I'm thankful for:

_____
_____
_____
_____
_____
_____

notes

For he satisfieth the longing soul, and filleth the hungry soul with goodness.—Psalm 107:9

TODAY'S A
WONDERFUL DAY

TODAY'S DATE _____ / _____ / _____

notes

passage I read:

_____
_____
_____
_____
_____
_____
_____

truths for my day:

_____
_____
_____
_____
_____
_____
_____

today I'm thankful for:

_____
_____
_____
_____
_____

The LORD is good to all: and his tender mercies are over all his works.—Psalm 145:9

TODAY'S A
WONDERFUL DAY

TODAY'S DATE _____ / _____ / _____

passage I read:

_____

_____

_____

_____

_____

_____

_____

_____

truths for my day:

_____

_____

_____

_____

_____

_____

_____

_____

today I'm thankful for:

_____

_____

_____

_____

_____

notes

Teach me to do thy will; for thou art my God: thy spirit is good; lead me into the land of uprightness.—Psalm 143:10

TODAY'S A
WONDERFUL DAY

TODAY'S DATE _____ / _____ / _____

notes

passage I read:

_____
_____
_____
_____
_____
_____
_____

truths for my day:

_____
_____
_____
_____
_____
_____
_____

today I'm thankful for:

_____
_____
_____
_____
_____

For the Lord God is a sun and shield: the Lord will give grace and glory: no good thing will he withhold from them that walk uprightly.—Psalm 84:11

TODAY'S A WONDERFUL DAY

TODAY'S DATE _____ / _____ / _____

passage I read:

_____

_____

_____

_____

_____

_____

_____

_____

truths for my day:

_____

_____

_____

_____

_____

_____

_____

today I'm thankful for:

_____

_____

_____

_____

_____

notes

Praise ye the LORD. O give thanks unto the LORD; for he is good:
for his mercy endureth for ever.—Psalm 106:1

TODAY'S A
WONDERFUL DAY

TODAY'S DATE _____ / _____ / _____

notes

passage I read:

_____
_____
_____
_____
_____
_____
_____

truths for my day:

_____
_____
_____
_____
_____
_____
_____

today I'm thankful for:

_____
_____
_____
_____
_____

For the LORD is good; his mercy is everlasting; and his truth
endureth to all generations.—Psalm 100:5

TODAY'S A
WONDERFUL DAY

TODAY'S DATE _____ / _____ / _____

passage I read:

_____
_____
_____
_____
_____
_____
_____
_____

truths for my day:

_____
_____
_____
_____
_____
_____
_____

today I'm thankful for:

_____
_____
_____
_____
_____

notes

But it is good for me to draw near to God: I have put my trust in the Lord God,
that I may declare all thy works.—Psalm 73:28

TODAY'S A
WONDERFUL DAY

TODAY'S DATE _____ / _____ / _____

notes

passage I read:

_____

_____

_____

_____

_____

_____

_____

truths for my day:

_____

_____

_____

_____

_____

_____

_____

today I'm thankful for:

_____

_____

_____

_____

Oh how great is thy goodness, which thou hast laid up for them that fear thee; which thou hast wrought for them that trust in thee before the sons of men!—Psalm 31:19

TODAY'S A
WONDERFUL DAY

TODAY'S DATE _____ / _____ / _____

passage I read:

_____
_____
_____
_____
_____
_____
_____

truths for my day:

_____
_____
_____
_____
_____
_____
_____

today I'm thankful for:

_____
_____
_____
_____

notes

Blessed be the Lord God, the God of Israel, who only doeth wondrous things.—Psalm 72:18

TODAY'S A
WONDERFUL DAY

TODAY'S DATE _____ /_____ /_____

notes

passage I read:

_____
_____
_____
_____
_____
_____
_____

truths for my day:

_____
_____
_____
_____
_____
_____
_____

today I'm thankful for:

_____
_____
_____
_____

He restoreth my soul: he leadeth me in the paths of righteousness for his name's sake.—
Psalm 23:3

TODAY'S A
WONDERFUL DAY

TODAY'S DATE _____ / _____ / _____

passage I read:

_____

_____

_____

_____

_____

_____

_____

_____

_____

truths for my day:

_____

_____

_____

_____

_____

_____

_____

_____

today I'm thankful for:

_____

_____

_____

_____

_____

_____

notes

Be of good courage, and he shall strengthen your heart,
all ye that hope in the LORD.—Psalm 31:24

TODAY'S A
WONDERFUL DAY

TODAY'S DATE _____ /_____ /_____

notes

passage I read:

_____
_____
_____
_____
_____
_____
_____

truths for my day:

_____
_____
_____
_____
_____
_____

today I'm thankful for:

_____
_____
_____
_____

Thy testimonies are wonderful: therefore doth my soul keep them.—Psalm 119:129

TODAY'S A
WONDERFUL DAY

TODAY'S DATE _____ / _____ / _____

passage I read:

notes

_____

_____

_____

_____

_____

_____

_____

truths for my day:

_____

_____

_____

_____

_____

_____

today I'm thankful for:

_____

_____

_____

_____

_____

Fear thou not; for I am with thee: be not dismayed; for I am thy God: I will strengthen thee; yea,
I will help thee; yea, I will uphold thee with the right hand of my righteousness.—Isaiah 41:10

TODAY'S A
WONDERFUL DAY

TODAY'S DATE _____ / _____ / _____

notes

passage I read:

_____
_____
_____
_____
_____
_____
_____
_____

truths for my day:

_____
_____
_____
_____
_____
_____
_____
_____

today I'm thankful for:

_____
_____
_____
_____
_____
_____

He hath made his wonderful works to be remembered: the Lord *is
gracious and full of compassion.*—Psalm 111:4

TODAY'S A
WONDERFUL DAY

TODAY'S DATE _____ / _____ / _____

passage I read:

_____
_____
_____
_____
_____
_____
_____
_____

truths for my day:

_____
_____
_____
_____
_____
_____
_____

today I'm thankful for:

_____
_____
_____
_____
_____

notes

Surely goodness and mercy shall follow me all the days of my life: and I will dwell in the house of the Lord
*for ever.—*Psalm 23:6

TODAY'S A
WONDERFUL DAY

TODAY'S DATE _____ / _____ / _____

notes

passage I read:

_____
_____
_____
_____
_____
_____
_____
_____

truths for my day:

_____
_____
_____
_____
_____
_____
_____
_____

today I'm thankful for:

_____
_____
_____
_____
_____

Trust in the Lord, and do good; so shalt thou dwell in the land,
and verily thou shalt be fed.—Psalm 37:3

TODAY'S A
WONDERFUL DAY

TODAY'S DATE _____ / _____ / _____

passage I read:

notes

_____

_____

_____

_____

_____

_____

_____

_____

truths for my day:

_____

_____

_____

_____

_____

_____

_____

today I'm thankful for:

_____

_____

_____

_____

_____

*Hear me, O Lord; for thy lovingkindness is good: turn unto me according
to the multitude of thy tender mercies.*—Psalm 69:16

TODAY'S A
WONDERFUL DAY

TODAY'S DATE _____ / _____ / _____

notes

passage I read:

_____
_____
_____
_____
_____
_____
_____
_____

truths for my day:

_____
_____
_____
_____
_____
_____
_____

today I'm thankful for:

_____
_____
_____
_____
_____

Lead me in thy truth, and teach me: for thou art the God of my salvation;
on thee do I wait all the day.—Psalm 25:5

TODAY'S A
WONDERFUL DAY

TODAY'S DATE _____ /_____ /_____

passage I read:

_____
_____
_____
_____
_____
_____
_____
_____

truths for my day:

_____
_____
_____
_____
_____
_____
_____

today I'm thankful for:

_____
_____
_____
_____
_____

notes

O taste and see that the LORD is good: blessed is the man that trusteth in him.—Psalm 34:8

TODAY'S A
WONDERFUL DAY

TODAY'S DATE _____ / _____ / _____

notes

passage I read:

_____
_____
_____
_____
_____
_____
_____
_____

truths for my day:

_____
_____
_____
_____
_____
_____
_____

today I'm thankful for:

_____
_____
_____
_____

One thing have I desired of the LORD, that will I seek after; that I may dwell in the house of the LORD all the days of my life, to behold the beauty of the LORD, and to enquire in his temple.—Psalm 27:4

TODAY'S A
WONDERFUL DAY

TODAY'S DATE _____ / _____ / _____

passage I read:

_____
_____
_____
_____
_____
_____
_____
_____

truths for my day:

_____
_____
_____
_____
_____
_____
_____

today I'm thankful for:

_____
_____
_____
_____
_____

notes

All the paths of the LORD are mercy and truth unto such as keep
his covenant and his testimonies.—Psalm 25:10

TODAY'S A
WONDERFUL DAY

TODAY'S DATE _____ / _____ / _____

notes

passage I read:

_____
_____
_____
_____
_____
_____
_____

truths for my day:

_____
_____
_____
_____
_____
_____

today I'm thankful for:

_____
_____
_____
_____
_____

Unto thee, O God, do we give thanks, unto thee do we give thanks: for that thy name is near thy wondrous works declare.—Psalm 75:1

TODAY'S A
WONDERFUL DAY

TODAY'S DATE _____ / _____ / _____

passage I read:

_____

_____

_____

_____

_____

_____

_____

_____

truths for my day:

_____

_____

_____

_____

_____

_____

_____

_____

today I'm thankful for:

_____

_____

_____

_____

_____

_____

notes

And my tongue shall speak of thy righteousness and of thy praise all the day long.—Psalm 35:28

TODAY'S A
WONDERFUL DAY

TODAY'S DATE _____ / _____ / _____

notes

passage I read:

_____
_____
_____
_____
_____
_____
_____

truths for my day:

_____
_____
_____
_____
_____
_____
_____

today I'm thankful for:

_____
_____
_____
_____
_____

Yet the LORD will command his lovingkindness in the day time, and in the night his song shall be with me, and my prayer unto the God of my life.—Psalm 42:8

TODAY'S A
WONDERFUL DAY

TODAY'S DATE _____ / _____ / _____

passage I read:

_____

_____

_____

_____

_____

_____

_____

truths for my day:

_____

_____

_____

_____

_____

_____

today I'm thankful for:

_____

_____

_____

_____

notes

And call upon me in the day of trouble: I will deliver thee, and thou shalt glorify me.—Psalm 50:15

TODAY'S A
WONDERFUL DAY

TODAY'S DATE _____ / _____ / _____

notes

passage I read:

_____
_____
_____
_____
_____
_____
_____

truths for my day:

_____
_____
_____
_____
_____
_____
_____

today I'm thankful for:

_____
_____
_____
_____

God is our refuge and strength, a very present help in trouble. Therefore will not we fear, though the earth be removed, and though the mountains be carried into the midst of the sea; Though the waters thereof roar and be troubled, though the mountains shake with the swelling thereof. Selah.—Psalm 46:1–3

TODAY'S A
WONDERFUL DAY

TODAY'S DATE _____ / _____ / _____

passage I read:

_____

_____

_____

_____

_____

_____

_____

truths for my day:

_____

_____

_____

_____

_____

_____

_____

today I'm thankful for:

_____

_____

_____

_____

_____

notes

Make me to understand the way of thy precepts: so shall I talk of thy wondrous works.—Psalm 119:27

TODAY'S A
WONDERFUL DAY

TODAY'S DATE _____ /_____ /_____

notes

passage I read:

truths for my day:

today I'm thankful for:

For thou art great, and doest wondrous things: thou art God alone.—Psalm 86:10

TODAY'S A
WONDERFUL DAY

TODAY'S DATE _____ / _____ / _____

passage I read:

_____
_____
_____
_____
_____
_____
_____
_____

truths for my day:

_____
_____
_____
_____
_____
_____
_____
_____

today I'm thankful for:

_____
_____
_____
_____
_____

notes

But I will sing of thy power; yea, I will sing aloud of thy mercy in the morning: for thou hast been my defence and refuge in the day of my trouble.—Psalm 59:16

TODAY'S A
WONDERFUL DAY

TODAY'S DATE _____ / _____ / _____

notes

passage I read:

_____

_____

_____

_____

_____

_____

_____

truths for my day:

_____

_____

_____

_____

_____

_____

_____

today I'm thankful for:

_____

_____

_____

_____

_____

Let my mouth be filled with thy praise and with thy honour all the day.—Psalm 71:8

TODAY'S A
WONDERFUL DAY

TODAY'S DATE _____ / _____ / _____

passage I read:

_____
_____
_____
_____
_____
_____
_____

truths for my day:

_____
_____
_____
_____
_____
_____

today I'm thankful for:

_____
_____
_____
_____
_____

notes

My tongue also shall talk of thy righteousness all the day long...—Psalm 71:24

TODAY'S A
WONDERFUL DAY

TODAY'S DATE _____ /_____ /_____

notes

passage I read:

_____
_____
_____
_____
_____
_____
_____

truths for my day:

_____
_____
_____
_____
_____
_____

today I'm thankful for:

_____
_____
_____
_____

I will speak of the glorious honour of thy majesty, and of thy
wondrous works.—Psalm 145:5

TODAY'S A
WONDERFUL DAY

TODAY'S DATE _____ / _____ / _____

passage I read:

_____

_____

_____

_____

_____

_____

_____

truths for my day:

_____

_____

_____

_____

_____

_____

_____

today I'm thankful for:

_____

_____

_____

_____

_____

notes

In the day of my trouble I will call upon thee: for thou wilt answer me. —Psalm 86:7

TODAY'S A
WONDERFUL DAY

TODAY'S DATE _____ / _____ / _____

notes

passage I read:

_____
_____
_____
_____
_____
_____
_____

truths for my day:

_____
_____
_____
_____
_____
_____
_____

today I'm thankful for:

_____
_____
_____
_____
_____

So teach us to number our days, that we may apply our hearts
unto wisdom.—Psalm 90:12

TODAY'S A
WONDERFUL DAY

TODAY'S DATE _____ / _____ / _____

passage I read:

_____
_____
_____
_____
_____
_____
_____
_____
_____

truths for my day:

_____
_____
_____
_____
_____
_____
_____
_____
_____

today I'm thankful for:

_____
_____
_____
_____
_____
_____

notes

Open thou mine eyes, that I may behold wondrous things out of thy law.—Psalm 119:18

TODAY'S A
WONDERFUL DAY

TODAY'S DATE _____ / _____ / _____

notes

passage I read:

_____
_____
_____
_____
_____
_____
_____
_____
_____

truths for my day:

_____
_____
_____
_____
_____
_____
_____
_____

today I'm thankful for:

_____
_____
_____
_____
_____

O satisfy us early with thy mercy; that we may rejoice and be glad all our days—Psalm 90:14

TODAY'S A
WONDERFUL DAY

TODAY'S DATE _____ / _____ / _____

passage I read:

_____

_____

_____

_____

_____

_____

_____

_____

truths for my day:

_____

_____

_____

_____

_____

_____

_____

_____

today I'm thankful for:

_____

_____

_____

_____

_____

notes

Sing unto the LORD, bless his name; shew forth his salvation
from day to day.—Psalm 96:2

TODAY'S A
WONDERFUL DAY

TODAY'S DATE _____ / _____ / _____

notes

passage I read:

truths for my day:

today I'm thankful for:

TODAY'S A WONDERFUL DAY

TODAY'S DATE _____ / _____ / _____

passage I read:

_____

_____

_____

_____

_____

_____

_____

truths for my day:

_____

_____

_____

_____

_____

_____

_____

today I'm thankful for:

_____

_____

_____

_____

_____

notes

This is the day which the LORD hath made; we will rejoice and be glad in it.—Psalm 118:24

TODAY'S A
WONDERFUL DAY

TODAY'S DATE _____ / _____ / _____

notes

passage I read:

_____
_____
_____
_____
_____
_____
_____
_____

truths for my day:

_____
_____
_____
_____
_____
_____
_____
_____

today I'm thankful for:

_____
_____
_____
_____

O how love I thy law! it is my meditation all the day.—Psalm 119:97

TODAY'S A
WONDERFUL DAY

TODAY'S DATE _____ / _____ / _____

passage I read:

_____

_____

_____

_____

_____

_____

_____

truths for my day:

_____

_____

_____

_____

_____

_____

_____

today I'm thankful for:

_____

_____

_____

_____

_____

notes

O God, thou hast taught me from my youth: and hitherto have I declared thy
wondrous works.—Psalm 71:17

TODAY'S A
WONDERFUL DAY

TODAY'S DATE _____ / _____ / _____

notes

passage I read:

....

....

....

....

....

....

truths for my day:

....

....

....

....

....

....

today I'm thankful for:

....

....

....

....

*In the day when I cried thou answeredst me, and strengthenedst me
with strength in my soul.*—Psalm 138:3

TODAY'S A
WONDERFUL DAY

TODAY'S DATE _____ / _____ / _____

passage I read:

_____

_____

_____

_____

_____

_____

_____

notes

truths for my day:

_____

_____

_____

_____

_____

_____

today I'm thankful for:

_____

_____

_____

_____

_____

Every day will I bless thee; and I will praise thy name for ever and ever.—Psalm 145:2

TODAY'S A
WONDERFUL DAY

TODAY'S DATE _____ / _____ / _____

notes

passage I read:

_____

_____

_____

_____

_____

_____

_____

truths for my day:

_____

_____

_____

_____

_____

_____

_____

today I'm thankful for:

_____

_____

_____

_____

_____

Casting all your care upon him; for he careth for you.—1 Peter 5:7

TODAY'S A
WONDERFUL DAY

TODAY'S DATE _____ / _____ / _____

passage I read:

_____
_____
_____
_____
_____
_____
_____
_____

truths for my day:

_____
_____
_____
_____
_____
_____
_____
_____

today I'm thankful for:

_____
_____
_____
_____
_____
_____

notes

But his delight is in the law of the LORD; and in his law doth he meditate day and night.—Psalm 1:2

TODAY'S A
WONDERFUL DAY

TODAY'S DATE _____ / _____ / _____

notes

passage I read:

_____

_____

_____

_____

_____

_____

_____

truths for my day:

_____

_____

_____

_____

_____

_____

_____

today I'm thankful for:

_____

_____

_____

_____

_____

I will praise thee; for I am fearfully and wonderfully made: marvellous are thy works; and that my soul knoweth right well.—Psalm 139:14

TODAY'S A
WONDERFUL DAY

TODAY'S DATE _____ / _____ / _____

passage I read:

_____

_____

_____

_____

_____

_____

_____

_____

truths for my day:

_____

_____

_____

_____

_____

_____

today I'm thankful for:

_____

_____

_____

_____

_____

notes

Good and upright is the LORD: therefore will he teach sinners in the way.—Psalm 25:8

TODAY'S A
WONDERFUL DAY

TODAY'S DATE _____/_____/_____

notes

passage I read:

_____
_____
_____
_____
_____
_____
_____

truths for my day:

_____
_____
_____
_____
_____
_____
_____

today I'm thankful for:

_____
_____
_____
_____
_____

Thou wilt keep him in perfect peace, whose mind is stayed on thee:
because he trusteth in thee.—Isaiah 26:3

TODAY'S A
WONDERFUL DAY

TODAY'S DATE _____ / _____ / _____

passage I read:

_____

_____

_____

_____

_____

_____

_____

truths for my day:

_____

_____

_____

_____

_____

_____

today I'm thankful for:

_____

_____

_____

_____

notes

*I had fainted, unless I had believed to see the goodness of the LORD in the
land of the living.*—Psalm 27:13

TODAY'S A
WONDERFUL DAY

TODAY'S DATE _____ / _____ / _____

notes

passage I read:

_____
_____
_____
_____
_____
_____
_____
_____

truths for my day:

_____
_____
_____
_____
_____
_____
_____

today I'm thankful for:

_____
_____
_____
_____
_____

The LORD hear thee in the day of trouble; the name of the God of
Jacob defend thee;—Psalm 20:1

TODAY'S A WONDERFUL DAY

TODAY'S DATE _____ / _____ / _____

passage I read:

_____

_____

_____

_____

_____

_____

_____

truths for my day:

_____

_____

_____

_____

_____

_____

_____

today I'm thankful for:

_____

_____

_____

_____

notes

Oh that men would praise the LORD for his goodness, and for his wonderful works to the children of men!—Psalm 107:8

TODAY'S A
WONDERFUL DAY

TODAY'S DATE _____ / _____ / _____

notes

passage I read:

_____
_____
_____
_____
_____
_____
_____

truths for my day:

_____
_____
_____
_____
_____
_____

today I'm thankful for:

_____
_____
_____
_____
_____

Trust in the LORD with all thine heart; and lean not unto thine own understanding. In all thy ways acknowledge him, and he shall direct thy paths.—Proverbs 3:5–6

TODAY'S A
WONDERFUL DAY

TODAY'S DATE _____ / _____ / _____

passage I read:

notes

_____
_____
_____
_____
_____
_____
_____
_____

truths for my day:

_____
_____
_____
_____
_____
_____
_____
_____

today I'm thankful for:

_____
_____
_____
_____
_____

Peace I leave with you, my peace I give unto you: not as the world giveth, give I unto you.
Let not your heart be troubled, neither let it be afraid.—John 14:27

TODAY'S A
WONDERFUL DAY

TODAY'S DATE _____ / _____ / _____

notes

passage I read:

_____

_____

_____

_____

_____

_____

_____

_____

truths for my day:

_____

_____

_____

_____

_____

_____

_____

today I'm thankful for:

_____

_____

_____

_____

*For I know the thoughts that I think toward you, saith the Lord, thoughts of peace,
and not of evil, to give you an expected end.*—Jeremiah 29:11

TODAY'S A
WONDERFUL DAY

TODAY'S DATE _____ / _____ / _____

passage I read:

_____
_____
_____
_____
_____
_____
_____
_____

truths for my day:

_____
_____
_____
_____
_____
_____
_____
_____

today I'm thankful for:

_____
_____
_____
_____
_____

notes

Many, O LORD my God, are thy wonderful works which thou hast done, and thy
thoughts which are to us-ward: they cannot be reckoned up in order unto thee: if I would
declare and speak of them, they are more than can be numbered.—Psalm 40:5

TODAY'S A
WONDERFUL DAY

TODAY'S DATE _____ / _____ / _____

notes

passage I read:

_____
_____
_____
_____
_____
_____
_____

truths for my day:

_____
_____
_____
_____
_____
_____
_____

today I'm thankful for:

_____
_____
_____
_____
_____

Praise the LORD; for the LORD is good: sing praises unto his name;
for it is pleasant.—Psalm 135:3

TODAY'S A
WONDERFUL DAY

TODAY'S DATE _____ / _____ / _____

passage I read:

_____
_____
_____
_____
_____
_____
_____
_____
_____

truths for my day:

_____
_____
_____
_____
_____
_____
_____
_____

today I'm thankful for:

_____
_____
_____
_____
_____
_____

notes

For he satisfieth the longing soul, and filleth the hungry soul with goodness.—Psalm 107:9

TODAY'S A
WONDERFUL DAY

TODAY'S DATE _____ / _____ / _____

notes

passage I read:

_____
_____
_____
_____
_____
_____
_____
_____

truths for my day:

_____
_____
_____
_____
_____
_____
_____
_____

today I'm thankful for:

_____
_____
_____
_____
_____
_____

The LORD is good to all: and his tender mercies are over all his works.—Psalm 145:9

TODAY'S A
WONDERFUL DAY

TODAY'S DATE _____ / _____ / _____

passage I read:

_____
_____
_____
_____
_____
_____
_____

truths for my day:

_____
_____
_____
_____
_____
_____

today I'm thankful for:

_____
_____
_____
_____

notes

Teach me to do thy will; for thou art my God: thy spirit is good; lead me into the land of uprightness. —Psalm 143:10

TODAY'S A
WONDERFUL DAY

TODAY'S DATE _____ / _____ / _____

notes

passage I read:

_____
_____
_____
_____
_____
_____
_____
_____

truths for my day:

_____
_____
_____
_____
_____
_____
_____

today I'm thankful for:

_____
_____
_____
_____
_____

For the Lord God is a sun and shield: the Lord will give grace and glory: no good thing will he withhold from them that walk uprightly.—Psalm 84:11

TODAY'S A
WONDERFUL DAY

TODAY'S DATE _____ / _____ / _____

passage I read:

_____

_____

_____

_____

_____

_____

_____

truths for my day:

_____

_____

_____

_____

_____

_____

today I'm thankful for:

_____

_____

_____

_____

notes

Praise ye the LORD. O give thanks unto the LORD; for he is good:
for his mercy endureth for ever.—Psalm 106:1

TODAY'S A
WONDERFUL DAY

TODAY'S DATE _____ /_____ /_____

notes

passage I read:

_____
_____
_____
_____
_____
_____
_____

truths for my day:

_____
_____
_____
_____
_____
_____

today I'm thankful for:

_____
_____
_____
_____

For the LORD is good; his mercy is everlasting; and his truth
endureth to all generations.—Psalm 100:5

TODAY'S A
WONDERFUL DAY

TODAY'S DATE _____ / _____ / _____

passage I read:

_____

_____

_____

_____

_____

_____

_____

_____

truths for my day:

_____

_____

_____

_____

_____

_____

_____

_____

today I'm thankful for:

_____

_____

_____

_____

_____

notes

*But it is good for me to draw near to God: I have put my trust in the Lord God,
that I may declare all thy works.*—Psalm 73:28

TODAY'S A
WONDERFUL DAY

TODAY'S DATE _____ / _____ / _____

notes

passage I read:

_____
_____
_____
_____
_____
_____
_____
_____

truths for my day:

_____
_____
_____
_____
_____
_____
_____

today I'm thankful for:

_____
_____
_____
_____
_____

Oh how great is thy goodness, which thou hast laid up for them that fear thee; which thou hast wrought for them that trust in thee before the sons of men!—Psalm 31:19

TODAY'S A
WONDERFUL DAY

TODAY'S DATE _____ / _____ / _____

passage I read:

_____
_____
_____
_____
_____
_____
_____
_____

truths for my day:

_____
_____
_____
_____
_____
_____
_____
_____

today I'm thankful for:

_____
_____
_____
_____
_____

notes

Blessed be the Lord God, the God of Israel, who only doeth wondrous things.—Psalm 72:18

TODAY'S A
WONDERFUL DAY

TODAY'S DATE _____ / _____ / _____

notes

passage I read:

truths for my day:

today I'm thankful for:

He restoreth my soul: he leadeth me in the paths of righteousness for his name's sake.—
Psalm 23:3

TODAY'S A
WONDERFUL DAY

TODAY'S DATE _____ / _____ / _____

passage I read:

_____
_____
_____
_____
_____
_____
_____
_____

truths for my day:

_____
_____
_____
_____
_____
_____
_____
_____

today I'm thankful for:

_____
_____
_____
_____
_____

notes

Be of good courage, and he shall strengthen your heart,
all ye that hope in the LORD. —Psalm 31:24

TODAY'S A
WONDERFUL DAY

TODAY'S DATE _____ /_____ /_____

notes

passage I read:

_____
_____
_____
_____
_____
_____
_____
_____

truths for my day:

_____
_____
_____
_____
_____
_____
_____
_____

today I'm thankful for:

_____
_____
_____
_____
_____

Thy testimonies are wonderful: therefore doth my soul keep them.—Psalm 119:129

TODAY'S A
WONDERFUL DAY

TODAY'S DATE _____ / _____ / _____

passage I read:

_____
_____
_____
_____
_____
_____
_____
_____

truths for my day:

_____
_____
_____
_____
_____
_____
_____

today I'm thankful for:

_____
_____
_____
_____
_____

notes

Fear thou not; for I am with thee: be not dismayed; for I am thy God: I will strengthen thee; yea,
I will help thee; yea, I will uphold thee with the right hand of my righteousness.—Isaiah 41:10

TODAY'S A
WONDERFUL DAY

TODAY'S DATE _____ / _____ / _____

notes

passage I read:

_____
_____
_____
_____
_____
_____
_____
_____

truths for my day:

_____
_____
_____
_____
_____
_____
_____
_____

today I'm thankful for:

_____
_____
_____
_____
_____

He hath made his wonderful works to be remembered: the LORD is
gracious and full of compassion.—Psalm 111:4

TODAY'S A
WONDERFUL DAY

TODAY'S DATE _____ / _____ / _____

passage I read:

_____

_____

_____

_____

_____

_____

_____

_____

truths for my day:

_____

_____

_____

_____

_____

_____

today I'm thankful for:

_____

_____

_____

_____

_____

notes

Surely goodness and mercy shall follow me all the days of my life: and I will dwell in the house of the LORD for ever.—Psalm 23:6

TODAY'S A
WONDERFUL DAY

TODAY'S DATE _____ / _____ / _____

notes

passage I read:

_____
_____
_____
_____
_____
_____
_____
_____

truths for my day:

_____
_____
_____
_____
_____
_____
_____

today I'm thankful for:

_____
_____
_____
_____
_____

*Trust in the LORD, and do good; so shalt thou dwell in the land,
and verily thou shalt be fed.*—Psalm 37:3

TODAY'S A
WONDERFUL DAY

TODAY'S DATE _____ / _____ / _____

passage I read:

_____

_____

_____

_____

_____

_____

_____

truths for my day:

_____

_____

_____

_____

_____

today I'm thankful for:

_____

_____

_____

_____

notes

Hear me, O LORD; for thy lovingkindness is good: turn unto me according
to the multitude of thy tender mercies.—Psalm 69:16

TODAY'S A
WONDERFUL DAY

TODAY'S DATE _____ / _____ / _____

notes

passage I read:

truths for my day:

today I'm thankful for:

Lead me in thy truth, and teach me: for thou art the God of my salvation;
on thee do I wait all the day.—Psalm 25:5

TODAY'S A
WONDERFUL DAY

TODAY'S DATE _____ / _____ / _____

passage I read:

_____
_____
_____
_____
_____
_____
_____
_____

truths for my day:

_____
_____
_____
_____
_____
_____

today I'm thankful for:

_____
_____
_____
_____
_____

notes

O taste and see that the LORD is good: blessed is the man that trusteth in him.—Psalm 34:8

TODAY'S A
WONDERFUL DAY

TODAY'S DATE _____ / _____ / _____

notes

passage I read:

_____
_____
_____
_____
_____
_____
_____
_____

truths for my day:

_____
_____
_____
_____
_____
_____
_____

today I'm thankful for:

_____
_____
_____
_____
_____

One thing have I desired of the LORD, that will I seek after; that I may dwell in the house of the LORD all the days of my life, to behold the beauty of the LORD, and to enquire in his temple.—Psalm 27:4

TODAY'S A
WONDERFUL DAY

TODAY'S DATE _____ / _____ / _____

passage I read:

_____

_____

_____

_____

_____

_____

_____

_____

truths for my day:

_____

_____

_____

_____

_____

_____

_____

today I'm thankful for:

_____

_____

_____

_____

_____

_____

notes

All the paths of the LORD are mercy and truth unto such as keep
his covenant and his testimonies.—Psalm 25:10

TODAY'S A
WONDERFUL DAY

TODAY'S DATE _____ /_____ /_____

notes

passage I read:

_____
_____
_____
_____
_____
_____
_____

truths for my day:

_____
_____
_____
_____
_____
_____

today I'm thankful for:

_____
_____
_____
_____

Unto thee, O God, do we give thanks, unto thee do we give thanks: for that thy name is near thy wondrous works declare.—Psalm 75:1

TODAY'S A
WONDERFUL DAY

TODAY'S DATE _____ / _____ / _____

passage I read:

_____
_____
_____
_____
_____
_____
_____
_____

truths for my day:

_____
_____
_____
_____
_____
_____
_____
_____

today I'm thankful for:

_____
_____
_____
_____
_____

notes

And my tongue shall speak of thy righteousness and of thy praise all the day long.—Psalm 35:28

TODAY'S A
WONDERFUL DAY

TODAY'S DATE _____ / _____ / _____

notes

passage I read:

_____
_____
_____
_____
_____
_____
_____
_____

truths for my day:

_____
_____
_____
_____
_____
_____
_____

today I'm thankful for:

_____
_____
_____
_____

Yet the LORD will command his lovingkindness in the day time, and in the night his song shall be with me,
and my prayer unto the God of my life.—Psalm 42:8

TODAY'S A
WONDERFUL DAY

TODAY'S DATE _____ / _____ / _____

passage I read:

_____

_____

_____

_____

_____

_____

_____

_____

truths for my day:

_____

_____

_____

_____

_____

_____

_____

today I'm thankful for:

_____

_____

_____

_____

_____

notes

And call upon me in the day of trouble: I will deliver thee, and thou shalt glorify me.—Psalm 50:15

TODAY'S A
WONDERFUL DAY

TODAY'S DATE _____ / _____ / _____

notes

passage I read:

_____
_____
_____
_____
_____
_____
_____

truths for my day:

_____
_____
_____
_____
_____
_____
_____

today I'm thankful for:

_____
_____
_____
_____
_____

God is our refuge and strength, a very present help in trouble. Therefore will not we fear, though the earth be removed, and though the mountains be carried into the midst of the sea; Though the waters thereof roar and be troubled, though the mountains shake with the swelling thereof. Selah.—Psalm 46:1–3

TODAY'S A
WONDERFUL DAY

TODAY'S DATE _____ / _____ / _____

passage I read:

_____
_____
_____
_____
_____
_____
_____
_____

truths for my day:

_____
_____
_____
_____
_____
_____
_____
_____

today I'm thankful for:

_____
_____
_____
_____
_____
_____

notes

Make me to understand the way of thy precepts: so shall I talk of thy wondrous works.—Psalm 119:27

TODAY'S A
WONDERFUL DAY

TODAY'S DATE _____ / _____ / _____

notes

passage I read:

_____
_____
_____
_____
_____
_____
_____
_____

truths for my day:

_____
_____
_____
_____
_____
_____
_____

today I'm thankful for:

_____
_____
_____
_____
_____

For thou art great, and doest wondrous things: thou art God alone.—Psalm 86:10

TODAY'S A
WONDERFUL DAY

TODAY'S DATE _____ / _____ / _____

passage I read:

_____
_____
_____
_____
_____
_____
_____
_____
_____

truths for my day:

_____
_____
_____
_____
_____
_____
_____
_____

today I'm thankful for:

_____
_____
_____
_____
_____
_____

notes

But I will sing of thy power; yea, I will sing aloud of thy mercy in the morning: for thou hast been my defence and refuge in the day of my trouble.—Psalm 59:16

TODAY'S A
WONDERFUL DAY

TODAY'S DATE _____ /_____ /_____

notes

passage I read:

_____
_____
_____
_____
_____
_____
_____
_____

truths for my day:

_____
_____
_____
_____
_____
_____
_____
_____

today I'm thankful for:

_____
_____
_____
_____
_____

Let my mouth be filled with thy praise and with thy honour all the day.—Psalm 71:8

TODAY'S A
WONDERFUL DAY

TODAY'S DATE _____ / _____ / _____

passage I read:

_____
_____
_____
_____
_____
_____
_____

truths for my day:

_____
_____
_____
_____
_____
_____
_____

today I'm thankful for:

_____
_____
_____
_____
_____

notes

My tongue also shall talk of thy righteousness all the day long...—Psalm 71:24

TODAY'S A
WONDERFUL DAY

TODAY'S DATE _____ / _____ / _____

notes

passage I read:

_____
_____
_____
_____
_____
_____
_____

truths for my day:

_____
_____
_____
_____
_____
_____
_____

today I'm thankful for:

_____
_____
_____
_____
_____

I will speak of the glorious honour of thy majesty, and of thy
wondrous works.—Psalm 145:5

TODAY'S A
WONDERFUL DAY

TODAY'S DATE _____ / _____ / _____

passage I read:

_____
_____
_____
_____
_____
_____
_____
_____
_____
_____

truths for my day:

_____
_____
_____
_____
_____
_____
_____
_____
_____

today I'm thankful for:

_____
_____
_____
_____
_____
_____

notes

In the day of my trouble I will call upon thee: for thou wilt answer me.—Psalm 86:7

TODAY'S A
WONDERFUL DAY

TODAY'S DATE _____ / _____ / _____

notes

passage I read:

_____
_____
_____
_____
_____
_____
_____
_____

truths for my day:

_____
_____
_____
_____
_____
_____
_____

today I'm thankful for:

_____
_____
_____
_____
_____

*So teach us to number our days, that we may apply our hearts
unto wisdom.*—Psalm 90:12

TODAY'S A
WONDERFUL DAY

TODAY'S DATE _____ /_____ /_____

passage I read:

notes

_____
_____
_____
_____
_____
_____
_____

truths for my day:

_____
_____
_____
_____
_____
_____
_____

today I'm thankful for:

_____
_____
_____
_____
_____

Open thou mine eyes, that I may behold wondrous things out of thy law.—Psalm 119:18

TODAY'S A
WONDERFUL DAY

TODAY'S DATE _____ / _____ / _____

notes

passage I read:

_____
_____
_____
_____
_____
_____
_____

truths for my day:

_____
_____
_____
_____
_____
_____
_____

today I'm thankful for:

_____
_____
_____
_____
_____

O satisfy us early with thy mercy; that we may rejoice and be glad all our days—Psalm 90:14

TODAY'S A
WONDERFUL DAY

TODAY'S DATE _____ /_____ /_____

passage I read:

_____

_____

_____

_____

_____

_____

_____

truths for my day:

_____

_____

_____

_____

_____

_____

today I'm thankful for:

_____

_____

_____

_____

notes

*Sing unto the LORD, bless his name; shew forth his salvation
from day to day.*—Psalm 96:2

TODAY'S A
WONDERFUL DAY

TODAY'S DATE _____ / _____ / _____

notes

passage I read:

_____
_____
_____
_____
_____
_____
_____
_____

truths for my day:

_____
_____
_____
_____
_____
_____
_____
_____

today I'm thankful for:

_____
_____
_____
_____
_____
_____

Sing unto him, sing psalms unto him: talk ye of all his
wondrous works.—Psalm 105:2

TODAY'S A WONDERFUL DAY

TODAY'S DATE _____ / _____ / _____

passage I read:

_____
_____
_____
_____
_____
_____
_____
_____
_____

truths for my day:

_____
_____
_____
_____
_____
_____
_____
_____
_____

today I'm thankful for:

_____
_____
_____
_____
_____
_____

notes

This is the day which the LORD hath made; we will rejoice and be glad in it. —Psalm 118:24

TODAY'S A
WONDERFUL DAY

TODAY'S DATE _____ / _____ / _____

notes

passage I read:

_____
_____
_____
_____
_____
_____
_____
_____

truths for my day:

_____
_____
_____
_____
_____
_____
_____
_____

today I'm thankful for:

_____
_____
_____
_____
_____

O how love I thy law! it is my meditation all the day.—Psalm 119:97

TODAY'S A
WONDERFUL DAY

TODAY'S DATE _____ / _____ / _____

passage I read:

_____
_____
_____
_____
_____
_____
_____
_____
_____

truths for my day:

_____
_____
_____
_____
_____
_____
_____

today I'm thankful for:

_____
_____
_____
_____
_____
_____

notes

O God, thou hast taught me from my youth: and hitherto have I declared thy wondrous works.—Psalm 71:17

TODAY'S A
WONDERFUL DAY

TODAY'S DATE _____ / _____ / _____

notes

passage I read:

_____
_____
_____
_____
_____
_____
_____
_____
_____

truths for my day:

_____
_____
_____
_____
_____
_____
_____

today I'm thankful for:

_____
_____
_____
_____
_____

*In the day when I cried thou answeredst me, and strengthenedst me
with strength in my soul.*—Psalm 138:3

TODAY'S A
WONDERFUL DAY

TODAY'S DATE _____ / _____ / _____

passage I read:

_____
_____
_____
_____
_____
_____
_____
_____

truths for my day:

_____
_____
_____
_____
_____
_____
_____
_____

today I'm thankful for:

_____
_____
_____
_____
_____
_____

notes

Every day will I bless thee; and I will praise thy name for ever and ever. —Psalm 145:2

TODAY'S A
WONDERFUL DAY

TODAY'S DATE _____ / _____ / _____

notes

passage I read:

_____
_____
_____
_____
_____
_____
_____
_____

truths for my day:

_____
_____
_____
_____
_____
_____
_____
_____

today I'm thankful for:

_____
_____
_____
_____
_____
_____

Casting all your care upon him; for he careth for you.—1 Peter 5:7

TODAY'S A
WONDERFUL DAY

TODAY'S DATE _____ / _____ / _____

passage I read:

_____
_____
_____
_____
_____
_____
_____
_____

truths for my day:

_____
_____
_____
_____
_____
_____
_____
_____

today I'm thankful for:

_____
_____
_____
_____
_____

notes

But his delight is in the law of the Lord; and in his law doth he meditate day and night.—Psalm 1:2

TODAY'S A
WONDERFUL DAY

TODAY'S DATE _____ / _____ / _____

notes

passage I read:

_____
_____
_____
_____
_____
_____
_____
_____

truths for my day:

_____
_____
_____
_____
_____
_____
_____
_____

today I'm thankful for:

_____
_____
_____
_____
_____
_____

I will praise thee; for I am fearfully and wonderfully made: marvellous are thy works; and that my soul knoweth right well.—Psalm 139:14

TODAY'S A
WONDERFUL DAY

TODAY'S DATE _____ / _____ / _____

passage I read:

_____

_____

_____

_____

_____

_____

_____

truths for my day:

_____

_____

_____

_____

_____

_____

today I'm thankful for:

_____

_____

_____

_____

_____

notes

Good and upright is the Lord: therefore will he teach sinners in the way.—Psalm 25:8

TODAY'S A
WONDERFUL DAY

TODAY'S DATE _____ / _____ / _____

notes

passage I read:

_____
_____
_____
_____
_____
_____
_____
_____

truths for my day:

_____
_____
_____
_____
_____
_____
_____

today I'm thankful for:

_____
_____
_____
_____
_____

Thou wilt keep him in perfect peace, whose mind is stayed on thee:
because he trusteth in thee.—Isaiah 26:3

TODAY'S A
WONDERFUL DAY

TODAY'S DATE _____ / _____ / _____

passage I read:

_____
_____
_____
_____
_____
_____
_____
_____

truths for my day:

_____
_____
_____
_____
_____
_____
_____

today I'm thankful for:

_____
_____
_____
_____
_____

notes

I had fainted, unless I had believed to see the goodness of the Lord in the land of the living.—Psalm 27:13

TODAY'S A
WONDERFUL DAY

TODAY'S DATE _____ / _____ / _____

notes

passage I read:

_____
_____
_____
_____
_____
_____
_____
_____

truths for my day:

_____
_____
_____
_____
_____
_____
_____

today I'm thankful for:

_____
_____
_____
_____
_____

The LORD hear thee in the day of trouble; the name of the God of
Jacob defend thee;—Psalm 20:1

TODAY'S A
WONDERFUL DAY

TODAY'S DATE _____ / _____ / _____

passage I read:

notes

_____
_____
_____
_____
_____
_____
_____
_____

truths for my day:

_____
_____
_____
_____
_____
_____
_____

today I'm thankful for:

_____
_____
_____
_____
_____

Oh that men would praise the LORD for his goodness, and for his wonderful works to the children of men!—Psalm 107:8

TODAY'S A
WONDERFUL DAY

TODAY'S DATE _____ / _____ / _____

notes

passage I read:

_____
_____
_____
_____
_____
_____
_____
_____

truths for my day:

_____
_____
_____
_____
_____
_____
_____

today I'm thankful for:

_____
_____
_____
_____
_____

Trust in the LORD with all thine heart; and lean not unto thine own understanding. In all thy ways acknowledge him, and he shall direct thy paths.—Proverbs 3:5–6

TODAY'S A
WONDERFUL DAY

TODAY'S DATE _____ /_____ /_____

passage I read:

_____
_____
_____
_____
_____
_____
_____
_____

truths for my day:

_____
_____
_____
_____
_____
_____
_____

today I'm thankful for:

_____
_____
_____
_____

notes

Peace I leave with you, my peace I give unto you: not as the world giveth, give I unto you.
Let not your heart be troubled, neither let it be afraid.—John 14:27

TODAY'S A
WONDERFUL DAY

TODAY'S DATE _____ / _____ / _____

notes

passage I read:

_____
_____
_____
_____
_____
_____
_____
_____

truths for my day:

_____
_____
_____
_____
_____
_____
_____
_____

today I'm thankful for:

_____
_____
_____
_____
_____

For I know the thoughts that I think toward you, saith the LORD, thoughts of peace,
and not of evil, to give you an expected end.—Jeremiah 29:11

TODAY'S A
WONDERFUL DAY

TODAY'S DATE _____ / _____ / _____

passage I read:

notes

_____
_____
_____
_____
_____
_____
_____
_____

truths for my day:

_____
_____
_____
_____
_____
_____
_____
_____

today I'm thankful for:

_____
_____
_____
_____

Many, O Lord my God, are thy wonderful works which thou hast done, and thy thoughts which are to us-ward: they cannot be reckoned up in order unto thee: if I would declare and speak of them, they are more than can be numbered.—Psalm 40:5

TODAY'S A
WONDERFUL DAY

TODAY'S DATE _____ / _____ / _____

notes

passage I read:

_____
_____
_____
_____
_____
_____

truths for my day:

_____
_____
_____
_____
_____
_____

today I'm thankful for:

_____
_____
_____
_____

Praise the LORD; for the LORD is good: sing praises unto his name;
for it is pleasant.—Psalm 135:3

TODAY'S A
WONDERFUL DAY

TODAY'S DATE _____ / _____ / _____

passage I read:

_____
_____
_____
_____
_____
_____
_____

truths for my day:

_____
_____
_____
_____
_____
_____
_____

today I'm thankful for:

_____
_____
_____
_____
_____

notes

For he satisfieth the longing soul, and filleth the hungry soul with goodness. —Psalm 107:9

TODAY'S A
WONDERFUL DAY

TODAY'S DATE _____ / _____ / _____

notes

passage I read:

_____
_____
_____
_____
_____
_____
_____

truths for my day:

_____
_____
_____
_____
_____
_____
_____
_____

today I'm thankful for:

_____
_____
_____
_____
_____

The Lord is good to all: and his tender mercies are over all his works.—Psalm 145:9

TODAY'S A
WONDERFUL DAY

TODAY'S DATE _____ / _____ / _____

passage I read:

_____
_____
_____
_____
_____
_____
_____
_____

truths for my day:

_____
_____
_____
_____
_____
_____
_____

today I'm thankful for:

_____
_____
_____
_____
_____

notes

Teach me to do thy will; for thou art my God: thy spirit is good; lead me into the land of uprightness.—Psalm 143:10

TODAY'S A
WONDERFUL DAY

TODAY'S DATE _____ / _____ / _____

notes

passage I read:

_____
_____
_____
_____
_____
_____
_____
_____

truths for my day:

_____
_____
_____
_____
_____
_____
_____
_____

today I'm thankful for:

_____
_____
_____
_____
_____

For the LORD God is a sun and shield: the LORD will give grace and glory: no good thing will he withhold from them that walk uprightly.—Psalm 84:11

TODAY'S A
WONDERFUL DAY

TODAY'S DATE _____ / _____ / _____

passage I read:

_____
_____
_____
_____
_____
_____
_____
_____
_____

truths for my day:

_____
_____
_____
_____
_____
_____
_____
_____

today I'm thankful for:

_____
_____
_____
_____
_____

notes

Praise ye the LORD. O give thanks unto the LORD; for he is good:
for his mercy endureth for ever.—Psalm 106:1

TODAY'S A WONDERFUL DAY

TODAY'S DATE _____ / _____ / _____

notes

passage I read:

_____

_____

_____

_____

_____

_____

_____

truths for my day:

_____

_____

_____

_____

_____

_____

_____

today I'm thankful for:

_____

_____

_____

_____

_____

For the Lord is good; his mercy is everlasting; and his truth
endureth to all generations.—Psalm 100:5

TODAY'S A
WONDERFUL DAY

TODAY'S DATE _____ / _____ / _____

passage I read:

_____
_____
_____
_____
_____
_____
_____
_____

truths for my day:

_____
_____
_____
_____
_____
_____
_____

today I'm thankful for:

_____
_____
_____
_____
_____

notes

But it is good for me to draw near to God: I have put my trust in the LORD God,
that I may declare all thy works.—Psalm 73:28

TODAY'S A
WONDERFUL DAY

TODAY'S DATE _____ / _____ / _____

notes

passage I read:

_____
_____
_____
_____
_____
_____
_____
_____
_____

truths for my day:

_____
_____
_____
_____
_____
_____
_____
_____
_____

today I'm thankful for:

_____
_____
_____
_____
_____

Oh how great is thy goodness, which thou hast laid up for them that fear thee; which thou hast wrought for them that trust in thee before the sons of men!—Psalm 31:19

TODAY'S A
WONDERFUL DAY

TODAY'S DATE _____ / _____ / _____

passage I read:

_____

_____

_____

_____

_____

_____

_____

_____

truths for my day:

_____

_____

_____

_____

_____

_____

today I'm thankful for:

_____

_____

_____

_____

_____

notes

Blessed be the Lord *God, the God of Israel, who only doeth wondrous things.*—Psalm 72:18

TODAY'S A
WONDERFUL DAY

TODAY'S DATE _____ / _____ / _____

notes

passage I read:

_____
_____
_____
_____
_____
_____
_____

truths for my day:

_____
_____
_____
_____
_____
_____
_____

today I'm thankful for:

_____
_____
_____
_____
_____

He restoreth my soul: he leadeth me in the paths of righteousness for his name's sake.—
Psalm 23:3

TODAY'S A
WONDERFUL DAY

TODAY'S DATE _____ / _____ / _____

passage I read:

_____
_____
_____
_____
_____
_____
_____
_____
_____

truths for my day:

_____
_____
_____
_____
_____
_____
_____
_____
_____

today I'm thankful for:

_____
_____
_____
_____
_____

notes

Be of good courage, and he shall strengthen your heart,
all ye that hope in the LORD. —Psalm 31:24

TODAY'S A WONDERFUL DAY

TODAY'S DATE _____ /_____ /_____

notes

passage I read:

_____
_____
_____
_____
_____
_____
_____
_____

truths for my day:

_____
_____
_____
_____
_____
_____
_____
_____

today I'm thankful for:

_____
_____
_____
_____
_____

Thy testimonies are wonderful: therefore doth my soul keep them.—Psalm 119:129

TODAY'S A
WONDERFUL DAY

TODAY'S DATE _____ /_____ /_____

passage I read:

_____

_____

_____

_____

_____

_____

_____

_____

notes

truths for my day:

_____

_____

_____

_____

_____

_____

_____

today I'm thankful for:

_____

_____

_____

_____

_____

Fear thou not; for I am with thee: be not dismayed; for I am thy God: I will strengthen thee; yea,
I will help thee; yea, I will uphold thee with the right hand of my righteousness.—Isaiah 41:10

TODAY'S A
WONDERFUL DAY

TODAY'S DATE _____ / _____ / _____

notes

passage I read:

_____
_____
_____
_____
_____
_____
_____
_____

truths for my day:

_____
_____
_____
_____
_____
_____
_____

today I'm thankful for:

_____
_____
_____
_____
_____

*He hath made his wonderful works to be remembered: the Lord is
gracious and full of compassion.—Psalm 111:4*

TODAY'S A
WONDERFUL DAY

TODAY'S DATE _____ / _____ / _____

passage I read:

notes

_____
_____
_____
_____
_____
_____
_____
_____

truths for my day:

_____
_____
_____
_____
_____
_____
_____

today I'm thankful for:

_____
_____
_____
_____
_____

Surely goodness and mercy shall follow me all the days of my life: and I will dwell in the house of the LORD for ever.—Psalm 23:6

TODAY'S A
WONDERFUL DAY

TODAY'S DATE _____ / _____ / _____

notes

passage I read:

_____
_____
_____
_____
_____
_____
_____

truths for my day:

_____
_____
_____
_____
_____
_____
_____

today I'm thankful for:

_____
_____
_____
_____
_____

*Trust in the Lord, and do good; so shalt thou dwell in the land,
and verily thou shalt be fed.*—Psalm 37:3

TODAY'S A
WONDERFUL DAY

TODAY'S DATE _____ / _____ / _____

passage I read:

notes

_____
_____
_____
_____
_____
_____
_____
_____

truths for my day:

_____
_____
_____
_____
_____
_____
_____
_____

today I'm thankful for:

_____
_____
_____
_____
_____
_____

*Hear me, O Lord; for thy lovingkindness is good: turn unto me according
to the multitude of thy tender mercies.*—Psalm 69:16

TODAY'S A
WONDERFUL DAY

TODAY'S DATE _____ / _____ / _____

notes

passage I read:

_____
_____
_____
_____
_____
_____
_____

truths for my day:

_____
_____
_____
_____
_____
_____
_____

today I'm thankful for:

_____
_____
_____
_____
_____

Lead me in thy truth, and teach me: for thou art the God of my salvation;
on thee do I wait all the day.—Psalm 25:5

TODAY'S A
WONDERFUL DAY

TODAY'S DATE _____ / _____ / _____

passage I read:

_____
_____
_____
_____
_____
_____
_____
_____
_____

truths for my day:

_____
_____
_____
_____
_____
_____
_____
_____
_____

today I'm thankful for:

_____
_____
_____
_____
_____
_____

notes

O taste and see that the LORD is good: blessed is the man that trusteth in him.—Psalm 34:8

TODAY'S A WONDERFUL DAY

TODAY'S DATE _____ / _____ / _____

notes

passage I read:

_____
_____
_____
_____
_____
_____
_____
_____

truths for my day:

_____
_____
_____
_____
_____
_____
_____

today I'm thankful for:

_____
_____
_____
_____

One thing have I desired of the LORD, that will I seek after; that I may dwell in the house of the LORD all the days of my life, to behold the beauty of the LORD, and to enquire in his temple.—Psalm 27:4

TODAY'S A
WONDERFUL DAY

TODAY'S DATE _____ / _____ / _____

passage I read:

notes

_____

_____

_____

_____

_____

_____

_____

_____

truths for my day:

_____

_____

_____

_____

_____

_____

_____

_____

today I'm thankful for:

_____

_____

_____

_____

_____

All the paths of the LORD are mercy and truth unto such as keep
his covenant and his testimonies.—Psalm 25:10

TODAY'S A
WONDERFUL DAY

TODAY'S DATE _____ / _____ / _____

notes

passage I read:

---

truths for my day:

---

today I'm thankful for:

Unto thee, O God, do we give thanks, unto thee do we give thanks: for that thy name is near thy wondrous works declare.—Psalm 75:1

TODAY'S A
WONDERFUL DAY

TODAY'S DATE _____ /_____ /_____

passage I read:

_____
_____
_____
_____
_____
_____
_____

truths for my day:

_____
_____
_____
_____
_____
_____
_____
_____

today I'm thankful for:

_____
_____
_____
_____
_____
_____

notes

And my tongue shall speak of thy righteousness and of thy praise all the day long.—Psalm 35:28

TODAY'S A
WONDERFUL DAY

TODAY'S DATE _____ / _____ / _____

notes

passage I read:

truths for my day:

today I'm thankful for:

Yet the Lord will command his lovingkindness in the day time, and in the night his song shall be with me,
and my prayer unto the God of my life.—Psalm 42:8

TODAY'S A
WONDERFUL DAY

TODAY'S DATE _____ /_____ /_____

passage I read:

_____
_____
_____
_____
_____
_____
_____

truths for my day:

_____
_____
_____
_____
_____
_____
_____

today I'm thankful for:

_____
_____
_____
_____
_____

notes

And call upon me in the day of trouble: I will deliver thee, and thou shalt glorify me.—Psalm 50:15

TODAY'S A WONDERFUL DAY

TODAY'S DATE _____ / _____ / _____

notes

passage I read:

_____
_____
_____
_____
_____
_____
_____
_____

truths for my day:

_____
_____
_____
_____
_____
_____
_____

today I'm thankful for:

_____
_____
_____
_____

God is our refuge and strength, a very present help in trouble. Therefore will not we fear, though the earth be removed, and though the mountains be carried into the midst of the sea; Though the waters thereof roar and be troubled, though the mountains shake with the swelling thereof. Selah.—Psalm 46:1–3

TODAY'S A
WONDERFUL DAY

TODAY'S DATE _____ / _____ / _____

passage I read:

notes

_____
_____
_____
_____
_____
_____
_____
_____

truths for my day:

_____
_____
_____
_____
_____
_____
_____
_____

today I'm thankful for:

_____
_____
_____
_____
_____

Make me to understand the way of thy precepts: so shall I talk of thy wondrous works.—Psalm 119:27

TODAY'S A
WONDERFUL DAY

TODAY'S DATE _____ / _____ / _____

notes

passage I read:

truths for my day:

today I'm thankful for:

For thou art great, and doest wondrous things: thou art God alone.—Psalm 86:10

TODAY'S A
WONDERFUL DAY

TODAY'S DATE _____ / _____ / _____

passage I read:

_____
_____
_____
_____
_____
_____
_____
_____

truths for my day:

_____
_____
_____
_____
_____
_____
_____
_____

today I'm thankful for:

_____
_____
_____
_____
_____
_____

But I will sing of thy power; yea, I will sing aloud of thy mercy in the morning: for thou hast been my defence and refuge in the day of my trouble.—Psalm 59:16

TODAY'S A
WONDERFUL DAY

TODAY'S DATE _____ /_____ /_____

notes

passage I read:

_____
_____
_____
_____
_____
_____
_____

truths for my day:

_____
_____
_____
_____
_____
_____
_____

today I'm thankful for:

_____
_____
_____
_____
_____

Let my mouth be filled with thy praise and with thy honour all the day.—Psalm 71:8

TODAY'S A
WONDERFUL DAY

TODAY'S DATE _____ /_____ /_____

passage I read:

_____
_____
_____
_____
_____
_____
_____

truths for my day:

_____
_____
_____
_____
_____
_____
_____

today I'm thankful for:

_____
_____
_____
_____
_____

notes

My tongue also shall talk of thy righteousness all the day long...—Psalm 71:24

TODAY'S A
WONDERFUL DAY

TODAY'S DATE _____ / _____ / _____

notes

passage I read:

_____
_____
_____
_____
_____
_____
_____

truths for my day:

_____
_____
_____
_____
_____
_____
_____

today I'm thankful for:

_____
_____
_____
_____

I will speak of the glorious honour of thy majesty, and of thy
wondrous works.—Psalm 145:5

TODAY'S A
WONDERFUL DAY

TODAY'S DATE _____ / _____ / _____

passage I read:

_____

_____

_____

_____

_____

_____

_____

_____

truths for my day:

_____

_____

_____

_____

_____

_____

_____

today I'm thankful for:

_____

_____

_____

_____

_____

notes

In the day of my trouble I will call upon thee: for thou wilt answer me. —Psalm 86:7

TODAY'S A
WONDERFUL DAY

TODAY'S DATE _____ / _____ / _____

notes

passage I read:

_____
_____
_____
_____
_____
_____
_____

truths for my day:

_____
_____
_____
_____
_____
_____
_____

today I'm thankful for:

_____
_____
_____
_____
_____

So teach us to number our days, that we may apply our hearts
unto wisdom.—Psalm 90:12

TODAY'S A
WONDERFUL DAY

TODAY'S DATE _____ / _____ / _____

passage I read:

_____

_____

_____

_____

_____

_____

_____

_____

truths for my day:

_____

_____

_____

_____

_____

_____

_____

_____

today I'm thankful for:

_____

_____

_____

_____

_____

notes

Open thou mine eyes, that I may behold wondrous things out of thy law.—Psalm 119:18

TODAY'S A
WONDERFUL DAY

TODAY'S DATE _____ / _____ / _____

notes

passage I read:

_____
_____
_____
_____
_____
_____
_____

truths for my day:

_____
_____
_____
_____
_____
_____
_____

today I'm thankful for:

_____
_____
_____
_____
_____

O satisfy us early with thy mercy; that we may rejoice and be glad all our days—Psalm 90:14

TODAY'S A
WONDERFUL DAY

TODAY'S DATE _____ / _____ / _____

passage I read:

_____
_____
_____
_____
_____
_____
_____
_____

truths for my day:

_____
_____
_____
_____
_____
_____
_____
_____

today I'm thankful for:

_____
_____
_____
_____
_____

notes

*Sing unto the LORD, bless his name; shew forth his salvation
from day to day.*—Psalm 96:2

TODAY'S A
WONDERFUL DAY

TODAY'S DATE _____ / _____ / _____

notes

passage I read:

_____

_____

_____

_____

_____

_____

_____

truths for my day:

_____

_____

_____

_____

_____

_____

_____

today I'm thankful for:

_____

_____

_____

_____

_____

Sing unto him, sing psalms unto him: talk ye of all his
wondrous works.—Psalm 105:2

TODAY'S A
WONDERFUL DAY

TODAY'S DATE _____ / _____ / _____

passage I read:

_____

_____

_____

_____

_____

_____

_____

_____

_____

truths for my day:

_____

_____

_____

_____

_____

_____

_____

_____

_____

today I'm thankful for:

_____

_____

_____

_____

_____

_____

notes

This is the day which the LORD hath made; we will rejoice and be glad in it.—Psalm 118:24

TODAY'S A
WONDERFUL DAY

TODAY'S DATE _____ /_____ /_____

notes

passage I read:

_____
_____
_____
_____
_____
_____
_____

truths for my day:

_____
_____
_____
_____
_____
_____
_____

today I'm thankful for:

_____
_____
_____
_____
_____

O how love I thy law! it is my meditation all the day.—Psalm 119:97

TODAY'S A
WONDERFUL DAY

TODAY'S DATE _____ / _____ / _____

passage I read:

_____
_____
_____
_____
_____
_____
_____
_____

truths for my day:

_____
_____
_____
_____
_____
_____
_____
_____

today I'm thankful for:

_____
_____
_____
_____

notes

O God, thou hast taught me from my youth: and hitherto have I declared thy
wondrous works.—Psalm 71:17

TODAY'S A
WONDERFUL DAY

TODAY'S DATE _____ / _____ / _____

notes

passage I read:

truths for my day:

today I'm thankful for:

*In the day when I cried thou answeredst me, and strengthenedst me
with strength in my soul.*—Psalm 138:3

TODAY'S A
WONDERFUL DAY

TODAY'S DATE _____ /_____ /_____

passage I read:

_____
_____
_____
_____
_____
_____
_____
_____

truths for my day:

_____
_____
_____
_____
_____
_____
_____
_____

today I'm thankful for:

_____
_____
_____
_____

notes

Every day will I bless thee; and I will praise thy name for ever and ever. —Psalm 145:2

TODAY'S A
WONDERFUL DAY

TODAY'S DATE _____ / _____ / _____

notes

passage I read:

_____
_____
_____
_____
_____
_____
_____
_____

truths for my day:

_____
_____
_____
_____
_____
_____
_____

today I'm thankful for:

_____
_____
_____
_____
_____

Casting all your care upon him; for he careth for you.—1 Peter 5:7

TODAY'S A
WONDERFUL DAY

TODAY'S DATE _____ /_____ /_____

passage I read:

_____

_____

_____

_____

_____

_____

_____

truths for my day:

_____

_____

_____

_____

_____

_____

today I'm thankful for:

_____

_____

_____

_____

_____

notes

But his delight is in the law of the LORD; and in his law doth he meditate day and night.—Psalm 1:2

TODAY'S A WONDERFUL DAY

TODAY'S DATE _____ / _____ / _____

notes

passage I read:

truths for my day:

today I'm thankful for:

I will praise thee; for I am fearfully and wonderfully made: marvellous are thy works; and that my soul knoweth right well.—Psalm 139:14

TODAY'S A
WONDERFUL DAY

TODAY'S DATE _____ / _____ / _____

passage I read:

notes

_____

_____

_____

_____

_____

_____

_____

_____

truths for my day:

_____

_____

_____

_____

_____

_____

_____

_____

today I'm thankful for:

_____

_____

_____

_____

_____

Good and upright is the LORD: therefore will he teach sinners in the way.—Psalm 25:8

TODAY'S A
WONDERFUL DAY

TODAY'S DATE _____ / _____ / _____

notes

passage I read:

_____

_____

_____

_____

_____

_____

_____

truths for my day:

_____

_____

_____

_____

_____

_____

today I'm thankful for:

_____

_____

_____

_____

_____

Thou wilt keep him in perfect peace, whose mind is stayed on thee:
because he trusteth in thee.—Isaiah 26:3

TODAY'S A
WONDERFUL DAY

TODAY'S DATE _____ / _____ / _____

passage I read:

_____

_____

_____

_____

_____

_____

_____

_____

notes

truths for my day:

_____

_____

_____

_____

_____

_____

today I'm thankful for:

_____

_____

_____

_____

_____

*I had fainted, unless I had believed to see the goodness of the LORD in the
land of the living.—Psalm 27:13*

TODAY'S A
WONDERFUL DAY

TODAY'S DATE _____ /_____ /_____

notes

passage I read:

_____
_____
_____
_____
_____
_____
_____

truths for my day:

_____
_____
_____
_____
_____
_____

today I'm thankful for:

_____
_____
_____
_____

The LORD hear thee in the day of trouble; the name of the God of
Jacob defend thee;—Psalm 20:1

TODAY'S A
WONDERFUL DAY

TODAY'S DATE _____ / _____ / _____

passage I read:

notes

_____

_____

_____

_____

_____

_____

_____

_____

truths for my day:

_____

_____

_____

_____

_____

_____

_____

_____

today I'm thankful for:

_____

_____

_____

_____

_____

Oh that men would praise the LORD for his goodness, and for his wonderful works to the children of men!—Psalm 107:8

TODAY'S A
WONDERFUL DAY

TODAY'S DATE _____ / _____ / _____

notes

passage I read:

_____
_____
_____
_____
_____
_____
_____

truths for my day:

_____
_____
_____
_____
_____
_____
_____

today I'm thankful for:

_____
_____
_____
_____

Trust in the Lord with all thine heart; and lean not unto thine own understanding. In all thy ways acknowledge him, and he shall direct thy paths.—Proverbs 3:5–6

TODAY'S A
WONDERFUL DAY

TODAY'S DATE _____ / _____ / _____

passage I read:

_____

_____

_____

_____

_____

_____

_____

_____

_____

_____

truths for my day:

_____

_____

_____

_____

_____

_____

_____

_____

today I'm thankful for:

_____

_____

_____

_____

_____

notes

Peace I leave with you, my peace I give unto you: not as the world giveth, give I unto you.
Let not your heart be troubled, neither let it be afraid.—John 14:27

TODAY'S A
WONDERFUL DAY

TODAY'S DATE _____ / _____ / _____

notes

passage I read:

truths for my day:

today I'm thankful for:

*For I know the thoughts that I think toward you, saith the LORD, thoughts of peace,
and not of evil, to give you an expected end.—Jeremiah 29:11*

TODAY'S A
WONDERFUL DAY

TODAY'S DATE _____ / _____ / _____

passage I read:

notes

_____
_____
_____
_____
_____
_____
_____
_____
_____

truths for my day:

_____
_____
_____
_____
_____
_____
_____
_____

today I'm thankful for:

_____
_____
_____
_____
_____

Many, O LORD my God, are thy wonderful works which thou hast done, and thy
thoughts which are to us-ward: they cannot be reckoned up in order unto thee: if I would
declare and speak of them, they are more than can be numbered.—Psalm 40:5

TODAY'S A
WONDERFUL DAY

TODAY'S DATE _____ / _____ / _____

notes

passage I read:

_____
_____
_____
_____
_____
_____
_____

truths for my day:

_____
_____
_____
_____
_____
_____
_____

today I'm thankful for:

_____
_____
_____
_____
_____

Praise the LORD; for the LORD is good: sing praises unto his name;
for it is pleasant.—Psalm 135:3

TODAY'S A
WONDERFUL DAY

TODAY'S DATE _____ / _____ / _____

passage I read:

_____
_____
_____
_____
_____
_____
_____

truths for my day:

_____
_____
_____
_____
_____
_____

today I'm thankful for:

_____
_____
_____
_____
_____

notes

For he satisfieth the longing soul, and filleth the hungry soul with goodness.—Psalm 107:9

TODAY'S A
WONDERFUL DAY

TODAY'S DATE _____ / _____ / _____

notes

passage I read:

_____
_____
_____
_____
_____
_____
_____
_____

truths for my day:

_____
_____
_____
_____
_____
_____
_____

today I'm thankful for:

_____
_____
_____
_____
_____

The LORD is good to all: and his tender mercies are over all his works.—Psalm 145:9

TODAY'S A
WONDERFUL DAY

TODAY'S DATE _____ / _____ / _____

passage I read:

_____

_____

_____

_____

_____

_____

_____

truths for my day:

_____

_____

_____

_____

_____

today I'm thankful for:

_____

_____

_____

_____

notes

Teach me to do thy will; for thou art my God: thy spirit is good; lead me into the land of uprightness.—Psalm 143:10

TODAY'S A
WONDERFUL DAY

TODAY'S DATE _____ / _____ / _____

notes

passage I read:

truths for my day:

today I'm thankful for:

For the LORD God is a sun and shield: the LORD will give grace and glory: no good thing will he withhold from them that walk uprightly. —Psalm 84:11

TODAY'S A WONDERFUL DAY

TODAY'S DATE _____ / _____ / _____

passage I read:

_____

_____

_____

_____

_____

_____

_____

_____

truths for my day:

_____

_____

_____

_____

_____

_____

_____

today I'm thankful for:

_____

_____

_____

_____

_____

notes

Praise ye the Lord. O give thanks unto the Lord; for he is good:
for his mercy endureth for ever.—Psalm 106:1

TODAY'S A
WONDERFUL DAY

TODAY'S DATE _____ / _____ / _____

notes

passage I read:

_____
_____
_____
_____
_____
_____
_____

truths for my day:

_____
_____
_____
_____
_____
_____
_____

today I'm thankful for:

_____
_____
_____
_____
_____

For the LORD is good; his mercy is everlasting; and his truth
endureth to all generations.—Psalm 100:5

TODAY'S A
WONDERFUL DAY

TODAY'S DATE _____ / _____ / _____

passage I read:

_____
_____
_____
_____
_____
_____
_____

truths for my day:

_____
_____
_____
_____
_____
_____

today I'm thankful for:

_____
_____
_____
_____
_____

notes

But it is good for me to draw near to God: I have put my trust in the Lord God, that I may declare all thy works.—Psalm 73:28

TODAY'S A
WONDERFUL DAY

TODAY'S DATE _____ / _____ / _____

notes

passage I read:

_____
_____
_____
_____
_____
_____
_____
_____

truths for my day:

_____
_____
_____
_____
_____
_____
_____

today I'm thankful for:

_____
_____
_____
_____

Oh how great is thy goodness, which thou hast laid up for them that fear thee; which thou hast wrought for them that trust in thee before the sons of men!—Psalm 31:19

TODAY'S A
WONDERFUL DAY

TODAY'S DATE _____ / _____ / _____

passage I read:

_____
_____
_____
_____
_____
_____
_____
_____

truths for my day:

_____
_____
_____
_____
_____
_____
_____

today I'm thankful for:

_____
_____
_____
_____
_____

notes

Blessed be the LORD God, the God of Israel, who only doeth wondrous things.—Psalm 72:18

TODAY'S A
WONDERFUL DAY

TODAY'S DATE _____ / _____ / _____

notes

passage I read:

_____
_____
_____
_____
_____
_____
_____

truths for my day:

_____
_____
_____
_____
_____
_____

today I'm thankful for:

_____
_____
_____
_____

He restoreth my soul: he leadeth me in the paths of righteousness for his name's sake.—
Psalm 23:3

TODAY'S A
WONDERFUL DAY

TODAY'S DATE _____ / _____ / _____

passage I read:

_____

_____

_____

_____

_____

_____

_____

truths for my day:

_____

_____

_____

_____

_____

_____

_____

today I'm thankful for:

_____

_____

_____

_____

notes

Be of good courage, and he shall strengthen your heart,
all ye that hope in the LORD.—Psalm 31:24

TODAY'S A
WONDERFUL DAY

TODAY'S DATE _____ / _____ / _____

notes

passage I read:

_____
_____
_____
_____
_____
_____
_____

truths for my day:

_____
_____
_____
_____
_____
_____
_____

today I'm thankful for:

_____
_____
_____
_____

Thy testimonies are wonderful: therefore doth my soul keep them.—Psalm 119:129

TODAY'S A
WONDERFUL DAY

TODAY'S DATE _____ / _____ / _____

passage I read:

_____
_____
_____
_____
_____
_____
_____
_____

truths for my day:

_____
_____
_____
_____
_____
_____
_____
_____

today I'm thankful for:

_____
_____
_____
_____
_____
_____

notes

*Fear thou not; for I am with thee: be not dismayed; for I am thy God: I will strengthen thee; yea,
I will help thee; yea, I will uphold thee with the right hand of my righteousness.*—Isaiah 41:10

TODAY'S A
WONDERFUL DAY

TODAY'S DATE _____ / _____ / _____

notes

passage I read:

_____
_____
_____
_____
_____
_____
_____

truths for my day:

_____
_____
_____
_____
_____
_____
_____

today I'm thankful for:

_____
_____
_____
_____

He hath made his wonderful works to be remembered: the Lord is
gracious and full of compassion.—Psalm 111:4

TODAY'S A
WONDERFUL DAY

TODAY'S DATE _____ / _____ / _____

passage I read:

notes

_____
_____
_____
_____
_____
_____
_____
_____

truths for my day:

_____
_____
_____
_____
_____
_____
_____
_____

today I'm thankful for:

_____
_____
_____
_____
_____
_____

Surely goodness and mercy shall follow me all the days of my life: and I will dwell in the house of the Lord
for ever.—Psalm 23:6

TODAY'S A
WONDERFUL DAY

TODAY'S DATE _____ / _____ / _____

notes

passage I read:

_____
_____
_____
_____
_____
_____
_____
_____

truths for my day:

_____
_____
_____
_____
_____
_____
_____

today I'm thankful for:

_____
_____
_____
_____
_____

*Trust in the LORD, and do good; so shalt thou dwell in the land,
and verily thou shalt be fed.*—Psalm 37:3

TODAY'S A
WONDERFUL DAY

TODAY'S DATE _____ / _____ / _____

passage I read:

_____
_____
_____
_____
_____
_____
_____
_____

truths for my day:

_____
_____
_____
_____
_____
_____

today I'm thankful for:

_____
_____
_____
_____

notes

Hear me, O LORD; for thy lovingkindness is good: turn unto me according to the multitude of thy tender mercies.—Psalm 69:16

TODAY'S A
WONDERFUL DAY

TODAY'S DATE _____ / _____ / _____

notes

passage I read:

truths for my day:

today I'm thankful for:

Lead me in thy truth, and teach me: for thou art the God of my salvation;
on thee do I wait all the day.—Psalm 25:5

TODAY'S A
WONDERFUL DAY

TODAY'S DATE _____ /_____ /_____

passage I read:

_____

_____

_____

_____

_____

_____

_____

truths for my day:

_____

_____

_____

_____

_____

_____

_____

today I'm thankful for:

_____

_____

_____

_____

_____

notes

O taste and see that the L ORD is good: blessed is the man that trusteth in him.—Psalm 34:8

TODAY'S A
WONDERFUL DAY

TODAY'S DATE _____ / _____ / _____

notes

passage I read:

_____
_____
_____
_____
_____
_____
_____

truths for my day:

_____
_____
_____
_____
_____
_____
_____

today I'm thankful for:

_____
_____
_____
_____
_____

One thing have I desired of the LORD, that will I seek after; that I may dwell in the house of the LORD all the days of my life, to behold the beauty of the LORD, and to enquire in his temple. —Psalm 27:4

TODAY'S A
WONDERFUL DAY

TODAY'S DATE _____ /_____ /_____

passage I read:

_____

_____

_____

_____

_____

_____

_____

truths for my day:

_____

_____

_____

_____

_____

_____

_____

today I'm thankful for:

_____

_____

_____

_____

_____

notes

All the paths of the LORD are mercy and truth unto such as keep
his covenant and his testimonies.—Psalm 25:10

TODAY'S A
WONDERFUL DAY

TODAY'S DATE _____ / _____ / _____

notes

passage I read:

truths for my day:

today I'm thankful for:

Unto thee, O God, do we give thanks, unto thee do we give thanks: for that thy name is near thy wondrous works declare.—Psalm 75:1

TODAY'S A
WONDERFUL DAY

TODAY'S DATE _____ / _____ / _____

passage I read:

notes

_____

_____

_____

_____

_____

_____

_____

_____

truths for my day:

_____

_____

_____

_____

_____

_____

_____

today I'm thankful for:

_____

_____

_____

_____

_____

And my tongue shall speak of thy righteousness and of thy praise all the day long.—Psalm 35:28

TODAY'S A
WONDERFUL DAY

TODAY'S DATE _____ / _____ / _____

notes

passage I read:

_____
_____
_____
_____
_____
_____
_____
_____
_____

truths for my day:

_____
_____
_____
_____
_____
_____
_____
_____

today I'm thankful for:

_____
_____
_____
_____
_____

Yet the LORD will command his lovingkindness in the day time, and in the night his song shall be with me, and my prayer unto the God of my life.—Psalm 42:8

TODAY'S A
WONDERFUL DAY

TODAY'S DATE _____ / _____ / _____

passage I read:

notes

_____

_____

_____

_____

_____

_____

_____

_____

truths for my day:

_____

_____

_____

_____

_____

_____

_____

today I'm thankful for:

_____

_____

_____

_____

_____

And call upon me in the day of trouble: I will deliver thee, and thou shalt glorify me.—Psalm 50:15

TODAY'S A
WONDERFUL DAY

TODAY'S DATE _____ / _____ / _____

notes

passage I read:

_____

_____

_____

_____

_____

_____

_____

truths for my day:

_____

_____

_____

_____

_____

_____

_____

today I'm thankful for:

_____

_____

_____

_____

_____

God is our refuge and strength, a very present help in trouble. Therefore will not we fear, though the earth be removed, and though the mountains be carried into the midst of the sea; Though the waters thereof roar and be troubled, though the mountains shake with the swelling thereof. Selah. —Psalm 46:1–3

TODAY'S A
WONDERFUL DAY

TODAY'S DATE _____ /_____ /_____

passage I read:

notes

_____

_____

_____

_____

_____

_____

_____

truths for my day:

_____

_____

_____

_____

_____

_____

today I'm thankful for:

_____

_____

_____

_____

_____

Make me to understand the way of thy precepts: so shall I talk of thy wondrous works.—Psalm 119:27

TODAY'S A
WONDERFUL DAY

TODAY'S DATE _____ / _____ / _____

notes

passage I read:

truths for my day:

today I'm thankful for:

For thou art great, and doest wondrous things: thou art God alone.—Psalm 86:10

TODAY'S A
WONDERFUL DAY

TODAY'S DATE _____ /_____ /_____

passage I read:

_____

_____

_____

_____

_____

_____

_____

_____

truths for my day:

_____

_____

_____

_____

_____

_____

_____

_____

today I'm thankful for:

_____

_____

_____

_____

_____

notes

But I will sing of thy power; yea, I will sing aloud of thy mercy in the morning: for thou hast been my defence and refuge in the day of my trouble.—Psalm 59:16

TODAY'S A
WONDERFUL DAY

TODAY'S DATE _____ / _____ / _____

notes

passage I read:

_____
_____
_____
_____
_____
_____
_____

truths for my day:

_____
_____
_____
_____
_____
_____
_____

today I'm thankful for:

_____
_____
_____
_____
_____

Let my mouth be filled with thy praise and with thy honour all the day. —Psalm 71:8

TODAY'S A
WONDERFUL DAY

TODAY'S DATE _____ / _____ / _____

passage I read:

_____
_____
_____
_____
_____
_____
_____

truths for my day:

_____
_____
_____
_____
_____
_____

today I'm thankful for:

_____
_____
_____
_____
_____

notes

My tongue also shall talk of thy righteousness all the day long...—Psalm 71:24

TODAY'S A
WONDERFUL DAY

TODAY'S DATE _____ /_____ /_____

notes

passage I read:

_____
_____
_____
_____
_____
_____

truths for my day:

_____
_____
_____
_____
_____
_____

today I'm thankful for:

_____
_____
_____
_____

I will speak of the glorious honour of thy majesty, and of thy
wondrous works.—Psalm 145:5

TODAY'S A
WONDERFUL DAY

TODAY'S DATE _____ / _____ / _____

passage I read:

_____

_____

_____

_____

_____

_____

_____

_____

truths for my day:

_____

_____

_____

_____

_____

_____

_____

today I'm thankful for:

_____

_____

_____

_____

_____

notes

In the day of my trouble I will call upon thee: for thou wilt answer me.—Psalm 86:7

TODAY'S A
WONDERFUL DAY

TODAY'S DATE _____ / _____ / _____

notes

passage I read:

_____
_____
_____
_____
_____
_____
_____

truths for my day:

_____
_____
_____
_____
_____
_____
_____

today I'm thankful for:

_____
_____
_____
_____

*So teach us to number our days, that we may apply our hearts
unto wisdom.—Psalm 90:12*

TODAY'S A WONDERFUL DAY

TODAY'S DATE _____ / _____ / _____

passage I read:

_____

_____

_____

_____

_____

_____

_____

_____

truths for my day:

_____

_____

_____

_____

_____

_____

today I'm thankful for:

_____

_____

_____

_____

notes

Open thou mine eyes, that I may behold wondrous things out of thy law.—Psalm 119:18

TODAY'S A
WONDERFUL DAY

TODAY'S DATE _____ / _____ / _____

notes

passage I read:

_____

_____

_____

_____

_____

_____

_____

truths for my day:

_____

_____

_____

_____

_____

_____

_____

today I'm thankful for:

_____

_____

_____

_____

O satisfy us early with thy mercy; that we may rejoice and be glad all our days—Psalm 90:14

TODAY'S A
WONDERFUL DAY

TODAY'S DATE _____ / _____ / _____

passage I read:

_____
_____
_____
_____
_____
_____
_____
_____

truths for my day:

_____
_____
_____
_____
_____
_____
_____

today I'm thankful for:

_____
_____
_____
_____
_____
_____

notes

Sing unto the LORD, bless his name; shew forth his salvation
from day to day.—Psalm 96:2

TODAY'S A
WONDERFUL DAY

TODAY'S DATE _____ / _____ / _____

notes

passage I read:

_____
_____
_____
_____
_____
_____
_____
_____

truths for my day:

_____
_____
_____
_____
_____
_____
_____

today I'm thankful for:

_____
_____
_____
_____
_____

Sing unto him, sing psalms unto him: talk ye of all his
wondrous works.—Psalm 105:2

TODAY'S A
WONDERFUL DAY

TODAY'S DATE _____ / _____ / _____

passage I read:

_____
_____
_____
_____
_____
_____
_____

truths for my day:

_____
_____
_____
_____
_____
_____
_____

today I'm thankful for:

_____
_____
_____
_____
_____

notes

This is the day which the LORD hath made; we will rejoice and be glad in it.—Psalm 118:24

TODAY'S A
WONDERFUL DAY

TODAY'S DATE _____ / _____ / _____

notes

passage I read:

_____
_____
_____
_____
_____
_____
_____

truths for my day:

_____
_____
_____
_____
_____
_____
_____

today I'm thankful for:

_____
_____
_____
_____

O how love I thy law! it is my meditation all the day.—Psalm 119:97

TODAY'S A
WONDERFUL DAY

TODAY'S DATE _____ /_____ /_____

passage I read:

notes

_____
_____
_____
_____
_____
_____
_____

truths for my day:

_____
_____
_____
_____
_____
_____
_____

today I'm thankful for:

_____
_____
_____
_____
_____
_____

O God, thou hast taught me from my youth: and hitherto have I declared thy
wondrous works.—Psalm 71:17

TODAY'S A
WONDERFUL DAY

TODAY'S DATE _____ / _____ / _____

notes

passage I read:

_____
_____
_____
_____
_____
_____

truths for my day:

_____
_____
_____
_____
_____
_____

today I'm thankful for:

_____
_____
_____
_____

In the day when I cried thou answeredst me, and strengthenedst me
with strength in my soul.—Psalm 138:3

TODAY'S A
WONDERFUL DAY

TODAY'S DATE _____ /_____ /_____

passage I read:

_____

_____

_____

_____

_____

_____

_____

truths for my day:

_____

_____

_____

_____

_____

today I'm thankful for:

_____

_____

_____

_____

notes

Every day will I bless thee; and I will praise thy name for ever and ever.—Psalm 145:2

TODAY'S A
WONDERFUL DAY

TODAY'S DATE _____ / _____ / _____

notes

passage I read:

_____
_____
_____
_____
_____
_____
_____
_____

truths for my day:

_____
_____
_____
_____
_____
_____
_____
_____

today I'm thankful for:

_____
_____
_____
_____
_____

Casting all your care upon him; for he careth for you.—1 Peter 5:7

TODAY'S A
WONDERFUL DAY

TODAY'S DATE _____ /_____ /_____

passage I read:

_____

_____

_____

_____

_____

_____

_____

_____

_____

truths for my day:

_____

_____

_____

_____

_____

_____

_____

_____

today I'm thankful for:

_____

_____

_____

_____

_____

notes

But his delight is in the law of the LORD; and in his law doth he meditate day and night.—Psalm 1:2

TODAY'S A
WONDERFUL DAY

TODAY'S DATE _____ / _____ / _____

notes

passage I read:

_____
_____
_____
_____
_____
_____
_____

truths for my day:

_____
_____
_____
_____
_____
_____
_____

today I'm thankful for:

_____
_____
_____
_____
_____

I will praise thee; for I am fearfully and wonderfully made: marvellous are thy works; and that my soul knoweth right well.—Psalm 139:14

TODAY'S A
WONDERFUL DAY

TODAY'S DATE _____ / _____ / _____

passage I read:

_____
_____
_____
_____
_____
_____
_____

truths for my day:

_____
_____
_____
_____
_____
_____
_____

today I'm thankful for:

_____
_____
_____
_____

notes

Good and upright is the Lord: therefore will he teach sinners in the way.—Psalm 25:8

TODAY'S A
WONDERFUL DAY

TODAY'S DATE _____ / _____ / _____

notes

passage I read:

_____
_____
_____
_____
_____
_____
_____

truths for my day:

_____
_____
_____
_____
_____
_____

today I'm thankful for:

_____
_____
_____
_____

Thou wilt keep him in perfect peace, whose mind is stayed on thee:
because he trusteth in thee.—Isaiah 26:3

TODAY'S A
WONDERFUL DAY

TODAY'S DATE _____ /_____ /_____

passage I read:

_____
_____
_____
_____
_____
_____
_____
_____

truths for my day:

_____
_____
_____
_____
_____
_____
_____

today I'm thankful for:

_____
_____
_____
_____
_____

notes

I had fainted, unless I had believed to see the goodness of the LORD in the land of the living. —Psalm 27:13

TODAY'S A
WONDERFUL DAY

TODAY'S DATE _____ / _____ / _____

notes

passage I read:

_____
_____
_____
_____
_____
_____
_____
_____

truths for my day:

_____
_____
_____
_____
_____
_____
_____
_____

today I'm thankful for:

_____
_____
_____
_____
_____

The LORD hear thee in the day of trouble; the name of the God of
Jacob defend thee;—Psalm 20:1

TODAY'S A
WONDERFUL DAY

TODAY'S DATE _____ / _____ / _____

passage I read:

_____

_____

_____

_____

_____

_____

_____

truths for my day:

_____

_____

_____

_____

_____

_____

_____

today I'm thankful for:

_____

_____

_____

_____

_____

notes

Oh that men would praise the LORD for his goodness, and for his wonderful works to the children of men!—Psalm 107:8

TODAY'S A WONDERFUL DAY

TODAY'S DATE _____ / _____ / _____

notes

passage I read:

_____
_____
_____
_____
_____
_____
_____

truths for my day:

_____
_____
_____
_____
_____
_____
_____

today I'm thankful for:

_____
_____
_____
_____
_____

Trust in the Lord with all thine heart; and lean not unto thine own understanding. In all thy ways acknowledge him, and he shall direct thy paths.—Proverbs 3:5–6

TODAY'S A
WONDERFUL DAY

TODAY'S DATE _____ / _____ / _____

passage I read:

_____
_____
_____
_____
_____
_____
_____
_____

truths for my day:

_____
_____
_____
_____
_____
_____
_____
_____

today I'm thankful for:

_____
_____
_____
_____
_____

notes

Peace I leave with you, my peace I give unto you: not as the world giveth, give I unto you.
Let not your heart be troubled, neither let it be afraid.—John 14:27

TODAY'S A
WONDERFUL DAY

TODAY'S DATE _____ /_____ /_____

notes

passage I read:

_____
_____
_____
_____
_____
_____
_____
_____

truths for my day:

_____
_____
_____
_____
_____
_____
_____
_____

today I'm thankful for:

_____
_____
_____
_____

For I know the thoughts that I think toward you, saith the LORD, thoughts of peace,
and not of evil, to give you an expected end.—Jeremiah 29:11

TODAY'S A
WONDERFUL DAY

TODAY'S DATE _____ / _____ / _____

passage I read:

_____

_____

_____

_____

_____

_____

_____

truths for my day:

_____

_____

_____

_____

_____

_____

today I'm thankful for:

_____

_____

_____

_____

_____

notes

Many, O Lord my God, are thy wonderful works which thou hast done, and thy thoughts which are to us-ward: they cannot be reckoned up in order unto thee: if I would declare and speak of them, they are more than can be numbered.—Psalm 40:5

TODAY'S A WONDERFUL DAY

TODAY'S DATE _____ / _____ / _____

notes

passage I read:

_____
_____
_____
_____
_____
_____
_____

truths for my day:

_____
_____
_____
_____
_____
_____
_____

today I'm thankful for:

_____
_____
_____
_____
_____

Praise the LORD; for the LORD is good: sing praises unto his name;
for it is pleasant.—Psalm 135:3

TODAY'S A
WONDERFUL DAY

TODAY'S DATE _____ / _____ / _____

passage I read:

notes

_____

_____

_____

_____

_____

_____

_____

_____

_____

truths for my day:

_____

_____

_____

_____

_____

_____

_____

_____

today I'm thankful for:

_____

_____

_____

_____

_____

For he satisfieth the longing soul, and filleth the hungry soul with goodness.—Psalm 107:9

TODAY'S A
WONDERFUL DAY

TODAY'S DATE _____ /_____ /_____

notes

passage I read:

_____
_____
_____
_____
_____
_____

truths for my day:

_____
_____
_____
_____
_____
_____

today I'm thankful for:

_____
_____
_____
_____

The LORD is good to all: and his tender mercies are over all his works.—Psalm 145:9

TODAY'S A
WONDERFUL DAY

TODAY'S DATE _____ /_____ /_____

passage I read:

notes

_____
_____
_____
_____
_____
_____
_____

truths for my day:

_____
_____
_____
_____
_____
_____
_____

today I'm thankful for:

_____
_____
_____
_____
_____

Teach me to do thy will; for thou art my God: thy spirit is good; lead me into the land of uprightness.—Psalm 143:10

TODAY'S A
WONDERFUL DAY

TODAY'S DATE _____/_____/_____

notes

passage I read:

_____
_____
_____
_____
_____
_____
_____

truths for my day:

_____
_____
_____
_____
_____
_____

today I'm thankful for:

_____
_____
_____
_____

For the LORD God is a sun and shield: the LORD will give grace and glory: no good thing will he withhold from them that walk uprightly.—Psalm 84:11

TODAY'S A
WONDERFUL DAY

TODAY'S DATE _____ / _____ / _____

passage I read:

_____

_____

_____

_____

_____

_____

_____

notes

truths for my day:

_____

_____

_____

_____

_____

_____

_____

today I'm thankful for:

_____

_____

_____

_____

_____

Praise ye the LORD. O give thanks unto the LORD; for he is good:
for his mercy endureth for ever.—Psalm 106:1

TODAY'S A
WONDERFUL DAY

TODAY'S DATE _____ /_____ /_____

notes

passage I read:

_____
_____
_____
_____
_____
_____
_____
_____

truths for my day:

_____
_____
_____
_____
_____
_____
_____

today I'm thankful for:

_____
_____
_____
_____
_____

*For the L*ORD *is good; his mercy is everlasting; and his truth*
endureth to all generations.—Psalm 100:5

TODAY'S A
WONDERFUL DAY

TODAY'S DATE _____ / _____ / _____

passage I read:

_____

_____

_____

_____

_____

_____

_____

truths for my day:

_____

_____

_____

_____

_____

_____

_____

today I'm thankful for:

_____

_____

_____

_____

notes

But it is good for me to draw near to God: I have put my trust in the LORD God,
that I may declare all thy works.—Psalm 73:28

TODAY'S A
WONDERFUL DAY

TODAY'S DATE _____ / _____ / _____

notes

passage I read:

_____
_____
_____
_____
_____
_____
_____

truths for my day:

_____
_____
_____
_____
_____
_____
_____

today I'm thankful for:

_____
_____
_____
_____
_____

Oh how great is thy goodness, which thou hast laid up for them that fear thee; which thou hast wrought for them that trust in thee before the sons of men!—Psalm 31:19

TODAY'S A
WONDERFUL DAY

TODAY'S DATE _____ / _____ / _____

passage I read:

_____
_____
_____
_____
_____
_____
_____

truths for my day:

_____
_____
_____
_____
_____
_____

today I'm thankful for:

_____
_____
_____
_____

notes

Blessed be the LORD God, the God of Israel, who only doeth wondrous things.—Psalm 72:18

TODAY'S A
WONDERFUL DAY

TODAY'S DATE _____ / _____ / _____

notes

passage I read:

_____
_____
_____
_____
_____
_____

truths for my day:

_____
_____
_____
_____
_____

today I'm thankful for:

_____
_____
_____

He restoreth my soul: he leadeth me in the paths of righteousness for his name's sake.—
Psalm 23:3

TODAY'S A
WONDERFUL DAY

TODAY'S DATE _____ / _____ / _____

passage I read:

_____

_____

_____

_____

_____

_____

_____

truths for my day:

_____

_____

_____

_____

_____

_____

today I'm thankful for:

_____

_____

_____

_____

_____

notes

Be of good courage, and he shall strengthen your heart,
all ye that hope in the LORD. —Psalm 31:24

TODAY'S A
WONDERFUL DAY

TODAY'S DATE _____ / _____ / _____

notes

passage I read:

_____
_____
_____
_____
_____
_____
_____
_____

truths for my day:

_____
_____
_____
_____
_____
_____
_____

today I'm thankful for:

_____
_____
_____
_____
_____

Thy testimonies are wonderful: therefore doth my soul keep them.—Psalm 119:129

TODAY'S A
WONDERFUL DAY

TODAY'S DATE _____ / _____ / _____

passage I read:

notes

_____
_____
_____
_____
_____
_____
_____
_____

truths for my day:

_____
_____
_____
_____
_____
_____
_____
_____

today I'm thankful for:

_____
_____
_____
_____
_____

Fear thou not; for I am with thee: be not dismayed; for I am thy God: I will strengthen thee; yea,
I will help thee; yea, I will uphold thee with the right hand of my righteousness.—Isaiah 41:10

TODAY'S A
WONDERFUL DAY

TODAY'S DATE _____ /_____ /_____

notes

passage I read:

_____
_____
_____
_____
_____
_____
_____

truths for my day:

_____
_____
_____
_____
_____
_____
_____

today I'm thankful for:

_____
_____
_____
_____

He hath made his wonderful works to be remembered: the LORD is
gracious and full of compassion.—Psalm 111:4

TODAY'S A
WONDERFUL DAY

TODAY'S DATE _____ /_____ /_____

passage I read:

_____
_____
_____
_____
_____
_____
_____
_____

truths for my day:

_____
_____
_____
_____
_____
_____
_____

today I'm thankful for:

_____
_____
_____
_____
_____

notes

Surely goodness and mercy shall follow me all the days of my life: and I will dwell in the house of the LORD for ever.—Psalm 23:6

TODAY'S A
WONDERFUL DAY

TODAY'S DATE _____ / _____ / _____

notes

passage I read:

_____
_____
_____
_____
_____
_____
_____

truths for my day:

_____
_____
_____
_____
_____
_____
_____

today I'm thankful for:

_____
_____
_____
_____
_____

*Trust in the LORD, and do good; so shalt thou dwell in the land,
and verily thou shalt be fed.—Psalm 37:3*

TODAY'S A
WONDERFUL DAY

TODAY'S DATE _____ / _____ / _____

passage I read:

_____

_____

_____

_____

_____

_____

_____

_____

_____

truths for my day:

_____

_____

_____

_____

_____

_____

_____

_____

_____

today I'm thankful for:

_____

_____

_____

_____

_____

_____

notes

*Hear me, O LORD; for thy lovingkindness is good: turn unto me according
to the multitude of thy tender mercies.*—Psalm 69:16

TODAY'S A
WONDERFUL DAY

TODAY'S DATE _____ / _____ / _____

notes

passage I read:

_____

_____

_____

_____

_____

_____

_____

_____

truths for my day:

_____

_____

_____

_____

_____

_____

_____

today I'm thankful for:

_____

_____

_____

_____

_____

Lead me in thy truth, and teach me: for thou art the God of my salvation;
on thee do I wait all the day.—Psalm 25:5

TODAY'S A
WONDERFUL DAY

TODAY'S DATE _____ / _____ / _____

passage I read:

_____
_____
_____
_____
_____
_____
_____
_____

truths for my day:

_____
_____
_____
_____
_____
_____
_____
_____

today I'm thankful for:

_____
_____
_____
_____
_____

notes

O taste and see that the LORD is good: blessed is the man that trusteth in him.—Psalm 34:8

TODAY'S A
WONDERFUL DAY

TODAY'S DATE _____ / _____ / _____

notes

passage I read:

_____
_____
....
_____
_____
....
_____
_____
....

truths for my day:

_____
....
_____
_____
....
_____
_____

today I'm thankful for:

....
_____
_____
....
_____

One thing have I desired of the LORD, that will I seek after; that I may dwell in the house of the LORD all the days of my life, to behold the beauty of the LORD, and to enquire in his temple.—Psalm 27:4

TODAY'S A
WONDERFUL DAY

TODAY'S DATE _____ / _____ / _____

passage I read:

_____

_____

_____

_____

_____

_____

_____

_____

truths for my day:

_____

_____

_____

_____

_____

_____

_____

today I'm thankful for:

_____

_____

_____

_____

_____

notes

All the paths of the LORD are mercy and truth unto such as keep
his covenant and his testimonies.—Psalm 25:10

TODAY'S A
WONDERFUL DAY

TODAY'S DATE _____ / _____ / _____

notes

passage I read:

_____

_____

_____

_____

_____

_____

_____

truths for my day:

_____

_____

_____

_____

_____

_____

_____

today I'm thankful for:

_____

_____

_____

_____

_____

Unto thee, O God, do we give thanks, unto thee do we give thanks: for that thy name is near thy wondrous works declare.—Psalm 75:1

TODAY'S A
WONDERFUL DAY

TODAY'S DATE _____ / _____ / _____

passage I read:

_____
_____
_____
_____
_____
_____
_____
_____

truths for my day:

_____
_____
_____
_____
_____
_____
_____

today I'm thankful for:

_____
_____
_____
_____
_____

notes

And my tongue shall speak of thy righteousness and of thy praise all the day long.—Psalm 35:28

TODAY'S A
WONDERFUL DAY

TODAY'S DATE _____ / _____ / _____

notes

passage I read:

_____
_____
_____
_____
_____
_____
_____

truths for my day:

_____
_____
_____
_____
_____
_____
_____

today I'm thankful for:

_____
_____
_____
_____

Yet the LORD will command his lovingkindness in the day time, and in the night his song shall be with me, and my prayer unto the God of my life.—Psalm 42:8

TODAY'S A WONDERFUL DAY

TODAY'S DATE _____ / _____ / _____

passage I read:

_____
_____
_____
_____
_____
_____
_____
_____

truths for my day:

_____
_____
_____
_____
_____
_____
_____

today I'm thankful for:

_____
_____
_____
_____
_____

notes

And call upon me in the day of trouble: I will deliver thee, and thou shalt glorify me.—Psalm 50:15

TODAY'S A
WONDERFUL DAY

TODAY'S DATE _____ / _____ / _____

notes

passage I read:

_____
_____
_____
_____
_____
_____
_____
_____

truths for my day:

_____
_____
_____
_____
_____
_____
_____
_____

today I'm thankful for:

_____
_____
_____
_____
_____

God is our refuge and strength, a very present help in trouble. Therefore will not we fear, though the earth be removed, and though the mountains be carried into the midst of the sea; Though the waters thereof roar and be troubled, though the mountains shake with the swelling thereof. Selah. —Psalm 46:1–3

TODAY'S A
WONDERFUL DAY

TODAY'S DATE _____ /_____ /_____

passage I read:

_____
_____
_____
_____
_____
_____
_____
_____

truths for my day:

_____
_____
_____
_____
_____
_____
_____
_____

today I'm thankful for:

_____
_____
_____
_____
_____
_____

notes

Make me to understand the way of thy precepts: so shall I talk of thy wondrous works.—Psalm 119:27

TODAY'S A
WONDERFUL DAY

TODAY'S DATE _____ / _____ / _____

notes

passage I read:

_____
_____
_____
_____
_____
_____
_____
_____

truths for my day:

_____
_____
_____
_____
_____
_____
_____
_____

today I'm thankful for:

_____
_____
_____
_____

For thou art great, and doest wondrous things: thou art God alone.—Psalm 86:10

TODAY'S A
WONDERFUL DAY

TODAY'S DATE _____ / _____ / _____

passage I read:

_____
_____
_____
_____
_____
_____
_____

truths for my day:

_____
_____
_____
_____
_____
_____
_____

today I'm thankful for:

_____
_____
_____
_____

notes

But I will sing of thy power; yea, I will sing aloud of thy mercy in the morning: for thou hast been my
defence and refuge in the day of my trouble.—Psalm 59:16

TODAY'S A
WONDERFUL DAY

TODAY'S DATE _____ / _____ / _____

notes

passage I read:

_____
_____
_____
_____
_____
_____
_____
_____

truths for my day:

_____
_____
_____
_____
_____
_____
_____
_____

today I'm thankful for:

_____
_____
_____
_____
_____

Let my mouth be filled with thy praise and with thy honour all the day.—Psalm 71:8

TODAY'S A
WONDERFUL DAY

TODAY'S DATE _____ / _____ / _____

passage I read:

_____
_____
_____
_____
_____
_____
_____
_____

truths for my day:

_____
_____
_____
_____
_____
_____
_____
_____

today I'm thankful for:

_____
_____
_____
_____
_____
_____

notes

My tongue also shall talk of thy righteousness all the day long...—Psalm 71:24

TODAY'S A
WONDERFUL DAY

TODAY'S DATE _____ /_____ /_____

notes

passage I read:

_____
_____
_____
_____
_____
_____
_____
_____

truths for my day:

_____
_____
_____
_____
_____
_____
_____
_____

today I'm thankful for:

_____
_____
_____
_____
_____

*I will speak of the glorious honour of thy majesty, and of thy
wondrous works.*—Psalm 145:5

TODAY'S A
WONDERFUL DAY

TODAY'S DATE _____ / _____ / _____

passage I read:

_____
_____
_____
_____
_____
_____
_____

truths for my day:

_____
_____
_____
_____
_____
_____
_____

today I'm thankful for:

_____
_____
_____
_____
_____

notes

In the day of my trouble I will call upon thee: for thou wilt answer me.—Psalm 86:7

TODAY'S A
WONDERFUL DAY

TODAY'S DATE _____ /_____ /_____

notes

passage I read:

_____
_____
_____
_____
_____
_____
_____
_____

truths for my day:

_____
_____
_____
_____
_____
_____
_____

today I'm thankful for:

_____
_____
_____
_____
_____

So teach us to number our days, that we may apply our hearts
unto wisdom.—Psalm 90:12

TODAY'S A
WONDERFUL DAY

TODAY'S DATE _____ /_____ /_____

passage I read:

_____

_____

_____

_____

_____

_____

_____

truths for my day:

_____

_____

_____

_____

_____

_____

_____

today I'm thankful for:

_____

_____

_____

_____

_____

notes

Open thou mine eyes, that I may behold wondrous things out of thy law.—Psalm 119:18

TODAY'S A
WONDERFUL DAY

TODAY'S DATE _____ /_____ /_____

notes

passage I read:

truths for my day:

today I'm thankful for:

O satisfy us early with thy mercy; that we may rejoice and be glad all our days—Psalm 90:14

TODAY'S A
WONDERFUL DAY

TODAY'S DATE _____ / _____ / _____

passage I read:

notes

_____

_____

_____

_____

_____

_____

_____

_____

truths for my day:

_____

_____

_____

_____

_____

_____

_____

today I'm thankful for:

_____

_____

_____

_____

_____

*Sing unto the LORD, bless his name; shew forth his salvation
from day to day.*—Psalm 96:2

TODAY'S A
WONDERFUL DAY

TODAY'S DATE _____ /_____ /_____

notes

passage I read:

_____
_____
_____
_____
_____
_____
_____
_____

truths for my day:

_____
_____
_____
_____
_____
_____
_____
_____

today I'm thankful for:

_____
_____
_____
_____
_____

*Sing unto him, sing psalms unto him: talk ye of all his
wondrous works.—Psalm 105:2*

TODAY'S A
WONDERFUL DAY

TODAY'S DATE _____ / _____ / _____

passage I read:

_____
_____
_____
_____
_____
_____
_____
_____

truths for my day:

_____
_____
_____
_____
_____
_____
_____
_____

today I'm thankful for:

_____
_____
_____
_____
_____

notes

This is the day which the LORD hath made; we will rejoice and be glad in it.—Psalm 118:24

TODAY'S A
WONDERFUL DAY

TODAY'S DATE _____ / _____ / _____

notes

passage I read:

_____
_____
_____
_____
_____
_____
_____

truths for my day:

_____
_____
_____
_____
_____
_____

today I'm thankful for:

_____
_____
_____
_____

O how love I thy law! it is my meditation all the day.—Psalm 119:97

TODAY'S A WONDERFUL DAY

TODAY'S DATE _____ / _____ / _____

passage I read:

notes

truths for my day:

today I'm thankful for:

O God, thou hast taught me from my youth: and hitherto have I declared thy
wondrous works.—Psalm 71:17

TODAY'S A
WONDERFUL DAY

TODAY'S DATE _____ / _____ / _____

notes

passage I read:

_____
_____
_____
_____
_____
_____
_____
_____
_____

truths for my day:

_____
_____
_____
_____
_____
_____
_____
_____

today I'm thankful for:

_____
_____
_____
_____
_____

In the day when I cried thou answeredst me, and strengthenedst me
with strength in my soul.—Psalm 138:3

TODAY'S A
WONDERFUL DAY

TODAY'S DATE _____ / _____ / _____

passage I read:

_____

_____

_____

_____

_____

_____

_____

_____

truths for my day:

_____

_____

_____

_____

_____

_____

today I'm thankful for:

_____

_____

_____

_____

_____

notes

Every day will I bless thee; and I will praise thy name for ever and ever.—Psalm 145:2

TODAY'S A
WONDERFUL DAY

TODAY'S DATE _____/_____/_____

notes

passage I read:

_____
_____
_____
_____
_____
_____
_____

truths for my day:

_____
_____
_____
_____
_____
_____
_____

today I'm thankful for:

_____
_____
_____
_____
_____

Casting all your care upon him; for he careth for you.—1 Peter 5:7

TODAY'S A
WONDERFUL DAY

TODAY'S DATE _____ / _____ / _____

passage I read:

_____

_____

_____

_____

_____

_____

_____

_____

truths for my day:

_____

_____

_____

_____

_____

_____

_____

today I'm thankful for:

_____

_____

_____

_____

_____

notes

But his delight is in the law of the LORD; and in his law doth he meditate day and night.—Psalm 1:2

TODAY'S A
WONDERFUL DAY

TODAY'S DATE _____ / _____ / _____

notes

passage I read:

_____
_____
_____
_____
_____
_____
_____
_____

truths for my day:

_____
_____
_____
_____
_____
_____
_____
_____

today I'm thankful for:

_____
_____
_____
_____
_____

I will praise thee; for I am fearfully and wonderfully made: marvellous are thy works; and that my soul knoweth right well.—Psalm 139:14

TODAY'S A
WONDERFUL DAY

TODAY'S DATE _____ / _____ / _____

passage I read:

_____

_____

_____

_____

_____

_____

_____

truths for my day:

_____

_____

_____

_____

_____

_____

_____

today I'm thankful for:

_____

_____

_____

_____

_____

notes

Good and upright is the LORD: therefore will he teach sinners in the way.—Psalm 25:8

TODAY'S A
WONDERFUL DAY

TODAY'S DATE _____ / _____ / _____

notes

passage I read:

truths for my day:

today I'm thankful for:

Thou wilt keep him in perfect peace, whose mind is stayed on thee:
because he trusteth in thee.—Isaiah 26:3

TODAY'S A
WONDERFUL DAY

TODAY'S DATE _____ / _____ / _____

passage I read:

_____
_____
_____
_____
_____
_____
_____

truths for my day:

_____
_____
_____
_____
_____
_____
_____

today I'm thankful for:

_____
_____
_____
_____
_____

notes

*I had fainted, unless I had believed to see the goodness of the LORD in the
land of the living.*—Psalm 27:13

TODAY'S A
WONDERFUL DAY

TODAY'S DATE _____ /_____ /_____

notes

passage I read:

truths for my day:

today I'm thankful for:

The LORD hear thee in the day of trouble; the name of the God of
Jacob defend thee;—Psalm 20:1

TODAY'S A
WONDERFUL DAY

TODAY'S DATE _____ / _____ / _____

passage I read:

_____
_____
_____
_____
_____
_____
_____

truths for my day:

_____
_____
_____
_____
_____
_____
_____

today I'm thankful for:

_____
_____
_____
_____

notes

Oh that men would praise the LORD for his goodness, and for his wonderful
works to the children of men!—Psalm 107:8

TODAY'S A
WONDERFUL DAY

TODAY'S DATE _____ /_____ /_____

notes

passage I read:

_____
_____
_____
_____
_____
_____
_____
_____

truths for my day:

_____
_____
_____
_____
_____
_____
_____
_____

today I'm thankful for:

_____
_____
_____
_____
_____

Trust in the LORD with all thine heart; and lean not unto thine own understanding. In all thy ways acknowledge him, and he shall direct thy paths.—Proverbs 3:5–6

TODAY'S A
WONDERFUL DAY

TODAY'S DATE _____ / _____ / _____

passage I read:

_____

_____

_____

_____

_____

_____

_____

truths for my day:

_____

_____

_____

_____

_____

_____

today I'm thankful for:

_____

_____

_____

_____

_____

notes

Peace I leave with you, my peace I give unto you: not as the world giveth, give I unto you.
Let not your heart be troubled, neither let it be afraid.—John 14:27

TODAY'S A
WONDERFUL DAY

TODAY'S DATE _____ / _____ / _____

notes

passage I read:

_____

_____

_____

_____

_____

_____

_____

_____

truths for my day:

_____

_____

_____

_____

_____

_____

_____

_____

today I'm thankful for:

_____

_____

_____

_____

_____

_____

For I know the thoughts that I think toward you, saith the Lord, thoughts of peace,
and not of evil, to give you an expected end.—Jeremiah 29:11

TODAY'S A
WONDERFUL DAY

TODAY'S DATE _____ / _____ / _____

passage I read:

_____
_____
_____
_____
_____
_____
_____
_____
_____

truths for my day:

_____
_____
_____
_____
_____
_____
_____
_____

today I'm thankful for:

_____
_____
_____
_____
_____

notes

Many, O Lord my God, are thy wonderful works which thou hast done, and thy thoughts which are to us-ward: they cannot be reckoned up in order unto thee: if I would declare and speak of them, they are more than can be numbered.—Psalm 40:5

TODAY'S A
WONDERFUL DAY

TODAY'S DATE _____ / _____ / _____

notes

passage I read:

_____
_____
_____
_____
_____
_____
_____
_____

truths for my day:

_____
_____
_____
_____
_____
_____
_____
_____

today I'm thankful for:

_____
_____
_____
_____
_____

Praise the Lord; *for the* Lord *is good: sing praises unto his name;*
for it is pleasant.—Psalm 135:3

TODAY'S A
WONDERFUL DAY

TODAY'S DATE _____ / _____ / _____

passage I read:

_____
_____
_____
_____
_____
_____
_____

truths for my day:

_____
_____
_____
_____
_____
_____
_____

today I'm thankful for:

_____
_____
_____
_____
_____

notes

For he satisfieth the longing soul, and filleth the hungry soul with goodness.—Psalm 107:9

TODAY'S A
WONDERFUL DAY

TODAY'S DATE _____ /_____ /_____

notes

passage I read:

_____
_____
_____
_____
_____
_____
_____

truths for my day:

_____
_____
_____
_____
_____
_____
_____

today I'm thankful for:

_____
_____
_____
_____
_____

The Lord is good to all: and his tender mercies are over all his works.—Psalm 145:9

TODAY'S A WONDERFUL DAY

TODAY'S DATE _____ / _____ / _____

passage I read:

_____

_____

_____

_____

_____

_____

_____

_____

truths for my day:

_____

_____

_____

_____

_____

_____

_____

_____

today I'm thankful for:

_____

_____

_____

_____

_____

notes

Teach me to do thy will; for thou art my God: thy spirit is good; lead me into the land of uprightness.—Psalm 143:10

TODAY'S A
WONDERFUL DAY

TODAY'S DATE _____ / _____ / _____

notes

passage I read:

_____
_____
_____
_____
_____
_____
_____
_____

truths for my day:

_____
_____
_____
_____
_____
_____
_____

today I'm thankful for:

_____
_____
_____
_____
_____

For the Lord God is a sun and shield: the Lord will give grace and glory: no good thing will he withhold from them that walk uprightly.—Psalm 84:11

TODAY'S A
WONDERFUL DAY

TODAY'S DATE _____ / _____ / _____

passage I read:

_____
_____
_____
_____
_____
_____
_____
_____

truths for my day:

_____
_____
_____
_____
_____
_____

today I'm thankful for:

_____
_____
_____
_____

notes

Praise ye the Lord. O give thanks unto the Lord; for he is good:
for his mercy endureth for ever.—Psalm 106:1

TODAY'S A
WONDERFUL DAY

TODAY'S DATE _____ / _____ / _____

notes

passage I read:

_____
_____
_____
_____
_____
_____
_____

truths for my day:

_____
_____
_____
_____
_____
_____
_____

today I'm thankful for:

_____
_____
_____
_____
_____

For the Lord is good; his mercy is everlasting; and his truth
endureth to all generations.—Psalm 100:5

TODAY'S A WONDERFUL DAY

TODAY'S DATE _____ / _____ / _____

passage I read:

_____
_____
_____
_____
_____
_____
_____
_____

truths for my day:

_____
_____
_____
_____
_____
_____
_____

today I'm thankful for:

_____
_____
_____
_____
_____

notes

But it is good for me to draw near to God: I have put my trust in the LORD God, that I may declare all thy works.—Psalm 73:28

TODAY'S A
WONDERFUL DAY

TODAY'S DATE _____ / _____ / _____

notes

passage I read:

_____
_____
_____
_____
_____
_____
_____
_____

truths for my day:

_____
_____
_____
_____
_____
_____
_____
_____

today I'm thankful for:

_____
_____
_____
_____
_____

Oh how great is thy goodness, which thou hast laid up for them that fear thee; which thou hast wrought for them that trust in thee before the sons of men!—Psalm 31:19

TODAY'S A
WONDERFUL DAY

TODAY'S DATE _____ / _____ / _____

passage I read:

_____

_____

_____

_____

_____

_____

_____

truths for my day:

_____

_____

_____

_____

_____

_____

today I'm thankful for:

_____

_____

_____

_____

_____

notes

Blessed be the LORD God, the God of Israel, who only doeth wondrous things. —Psalm 72:18

TODAY'S A
WONDERFUL DAY

TODAY'S DATE _____ / _____ / _____

notes

passage I read:

_____
_____
_____
_____
_____
_____
_____
_____

truths for my day:

_____
_____
_____
_____
_____
_____
_____

today I'm thankful for:

_____
_____
_____
_____
_____

He restoreth my soul: he leadeth me in the paths of righteousness for his name's sake.—
Psalm 23:3

TODAY'S A WONDERFUL DAY

TODAY'S DATE _____/_____/_____

passage I read:

_____
_____
_____
_____
_____
_____
_____
_____

truths for my day:

_____
_____
_____
_____
_____
_____
_____

today I'm thankful for:

_____
_____
_____
_____
_____

notes

*Be of good courage, and he shall strengthen your heart,
all ye that hope in the Lord.*—Psalm 31:24

TODAY'S A
WONDERFUL DAY

TODAY'S DATE _____ /_____ /_____

notes

passage I read:

_____
_____
_____
_____
_____
_____
_____
_____

truths for my day:

_____
_____
_____
_____
_____
_____
_____

today I'm thankful for:

_____
_____
_____
_____

Thy testimonies are wonderful: therefore doth my soul keep them.—Psalm 119:129

TODAY'S A
WONDERFUL DAY

TODAY'S DATE _____ / _____ / _____

passage I read:

notes

_____
_____
_____
_____
_____
_____
_____
_____

truths for my day:

_____
_____
_____
_____
_____
_____
_____

today I'm thankful for:

_____
_____
_____
_____
_____

*Fear thou not; for I am with thee: be not dismayed; for I am thy God: I will strengthen thee; yea,
I will help thee; yea, I will uphold thee with the right hand of my righteousness.*—Isaiah 41:10

TODAY'S A
WONDERFUL DAY

TODAY'S DATE _____ / _____ / _____

notes

passage I read:

_____
_____
_____
_____
_____
_____
_____

truths for my day:

_____
_____
_____
_____
_____
_____
_____

today I'm thankful for:

_____
_____
_____
_____

*He hath made his wonderful works to be remembered: the LORD is
gracious and full of compassion.* —Psalm 111:4

TODAY'S A
WONDERFUL DAY

TODAY'S DATE _____ / _____ / _____

passage I read:

notes

_____
_____
_____
_____
_____
_____
_____
_____
_____

truths for my day:

_____
_____
_____
_____
_____
_____
_____
_____

today I'm thankful for:

_____
_____
_____
_____
_____

Surely goodness and mercy shall follow me all the days of my life: and I will dwell in the house of the LORD for ever.—Psalm 23:6

TODAY'S A
WONDERFUL DAY

TODAY'S DATE _____ / _____ / _____

notes

passage I read:

....
....
....
....
....
....
....
....

truths for my day:

....
....
....
....
....
....
....

today I'm thankful for:

....
....
....
....
....

*Trust in the LORD, and do good; so shalt thou dwell in the land,
and verily thou shalt be fed.—Psalm 37:3*

TODAY'S A
WONDERFUL DAY

TODAY'S DATE _____ / _____ / _____

passage I read:

_____
_____
_____
_____
_____
_____
_____
_____

truths for my day:

_____
_____
_____
_____
_____
_____
_____
_____

today I'm thankful for:

_____
_____
_____
_____
_____

notes

*Hear me, O LORD; for thy lovingkindness is good: turn unto me according
to the multitude of thy tender mercies.*—Psalm 69:16

TODAY'S A WONDERFUL DAY

TODAY'S DATE _____ / _____ / _____

notes

passage I read:

_____
_____
_____
_____
_____
_____
_____

truths for my day:

_____
_____
_____
_____
_____
_____
_____

today I'm thankful for:

_____
_____
_____
_____
_____

Lead me in thy truth, and teach me: for thou art the God of my salvation;
on thee do I wait all the day.—Psalm 25:5

Also available from
Striving Together Publications

It's a Wonderful Life
Serving God Joyfully in Marriage and Ministry

The pages of this book are a breath of fresh air for ladies who are tired
of trying to love their husbands and serve God in their own strength.
From the very first page, your heart will be uplifted by Terrie's candid,
humorous, and down-to-earth approach to loving God, supporting your
husband, and serving God's people both biblically and joyfully. You'll
find new joy and fresh strength as you delve into these pages. Discover
that it really is a "wonderful life" when your life is dedicated to Jesus
Christ! (280 pages, paperback)

strivingtogether.com

Also available from
Striving Together Publications

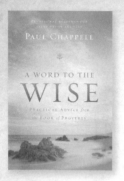

A Word to the Wise
In this power-packed daily devotional, each page shares a nugget of wisdom from the book of Proverbs. Written for the practically-minded Christian, each reading concludes with a distilled truth that you can immediately apply to your life. Let God's wisdom from the book of Proverbs equip you for the challenges of your daily life. (424 pages, hardback)

Sacred Motives
Sometimes in the midst of our service, we lose sight of why we do what we do. We slip into a pattern of empty routines or misguided ambition. In these pages, you will be challenged to take a thorough spiritual inventory—to allow the Holy Spirit of God to explore the deepest motives of your soul and reignite your passion to serve for what pleases Him. (144 pages, paperback)

Save the Day
Tucked into a less-known passage of Scripture is the story of an unnamed woman, simply referred to as "a wise woman." In a desperate moment, recorded in 2 Samuel 20, her wisdom saved the day for her hometown, the army of King David, and the entire nation of Israel. In these pages, learn practical lessons from this woman on gaining and using God's wisdom. (62 pages, mini paperback)

strivingtogether.com

Also available from
Striving Together Publications

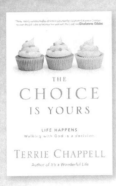

The Choice is Yours

We live in a culture that caters to our choices. They encourage us, "just follow your heart." God has given us a much better guide, however, in His Word. In *The Choice Is Yours*, Terrie Chappell leads readers through twelve choices that can strengthen or weaken your walk with God. (208 pages, paperback)

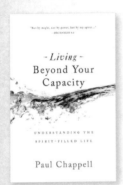

Living Beyond Your Capacity

The wonderful Holy Spirit of God desires to come into your life at salvation and unfold a daily work of power, grace, and transformation. He can enable you to live a supernatural life—a life that exceeds your human capacity. You can begin discovering and experiencing the Spirit-filled life today! (208 pages, paperback)

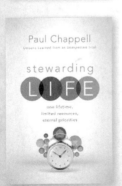

Stewarding Life

God has given you one life and filled it with resources—time, health, finances, relationships, influence, and more. How you steward these resources will determine whether you successfully fulfill God's eternal purpose for your life. This book will take you on a personal stewardship journey, equipping you to live effectively and biblically. (280 pages, hardback)

strivingtogether.com

Visit us online

strivingtogether.com

wcbc.edu